Privateε

DAVID SWARTS — BEST
WISHES FOR A GREAT TRIP
Thru History !

Ken Rossignol 3/25/13

TITANIC

1912

KEN ROSSIGNOL

A 21st century reporter's look back at the original news coverage of the 20th century's first major disaster

KEN ROSSIGNOL

Dedication

This book is dedicated to all those who lost their lives
on the *RMS Titanic*.

KEN ROSSIGNOL

TITANIC 1912

The Sphere: An Illustrated Newspaper for the Home) was a British newspaper, published weekly from 27 January 1900 until the closure of the paper on 27 June 1964; the first issue came out at the height of the Boer War and was no doubt a product of that conflict and the public appetite for images. At the time, it was in direct competition with *The Graphic* and *Illustrated London News*, and evidence of this rivalry

can be seen in the latter's publication shortly after of a new illustrated paper entitled *The Spear* in an attempt to confuse readers. During World War I, the weekly issues were called 'war numbers' and over two hundred appeared between 1914 and 1919. In all, it totaled 3,343 issues, plus a special supplement issued in December 1964, entitled *Winston Churchill: A Memorial Tribute*

In addition to *The Sphere*, this book is based on the news reporting of the *Times* of London, the *New York Times*, *The New York Evening World*, *The Los Angeles Times*, *The Washington Times*, *The Washington Post*, *The Baltimore American*, *The Richmond Times Dispatch*, *The New York Herald*, *The New York Tribune* and the *Chicago Times*. Thanks to Bruce M. Caplan, who is a world-class historian about the *Titanic*.

KEN ROSSIGNOL

TITANIC 1912

Chapter One – Breaking News

Just three months and a single day were all that separated the tragedy of the magnificent liner *RMS Titanic* in 1912 and that of a modern ship, the *Costa Concordia*, one hundred years later.

In both cases, the "press" as it used to be called, and the "media" as it is now commonly referred to, describes the various electronic and print sources of news coverage; and how they played an important role in the tragedies.

At about 11:40 pm on Sunday, April 14, 1912, the *RMS Titanic* arrived at a point in destiny with an iceberg, the fatal blow being struck underwater. At about 9:30 pm on Friday the 13th of January, 2012, the *Concordia* struck a large underwater rock which ripped a fatal gash into that ship.

Both instances could have been easily avoided by the masters of the ship.

Captain Edward J. Smith, the Admiral of the White Star Line was to retire after guiding the *Titanic* on its maiden voyage. The hapless captain of the Costa Concordia offered silly excuses for his venture close to shore which put his $450 million ship in jeopardy and cost the lives of 32 souls entrusted to his care. Captain Smith went down with his ship while Concordia's Captain Schettino claimed he fell into a lifeboat and now is under house arrest while authorities prepare to try him for his alleged crimes.

The *Titanic* disaster is one of the greatest stories ever told, retold and dramatized in musicals, movies, books and even sheet music.

There is little to add to the body of facts and much that could be added to sort out the misconceptions, myths and fabrications which have crept up over the years. Therefore, pointing out the former and sifting through the latter is the purpose of this effort. The approach here is to provide to the reader how news coverage of the *Titanic* was provided in the hours, days and weeks following the sinking of the ship and how or whether that coverage was efficient, tawdry or accurate --- or some strange combination of all three.

The era of "yellow journalism" was in full flower in 1912 when the *Titanic* set out from Southampton, England on April 10, 1912.

The first tool of communication at that time was the 'wireless' telegraph. How ironic that the most immediate tool at hand for a reporter one hundred years later is the 'wireless' telephone. With all the advances in technology, men walking on the moon, a space station and heart transplants seemingly routine, the most important communication devise for a breaking news story is still referred to as 'wireless'.

Two of the major players in the story of the *Titanic* had been adversaries for quite a while. William Randolph Hearst, owner of the Hearst syndicate of newspapers, already had been given credit for starting the Spanish-American War, or so some believe, and he had a chip on his shoulder for White Star Line President Bruce Ismay.

Ismay had taken over the shipping company which had been owned by his father and he arranged a deal with a large international company based in New Jersey – International Mercantile Marine. That company was part of the financial empire owned by J. Pierpont Morgan, a wealthy industrialist and banker who personified the "Gilded Age".

When Ismay's great liner met her doom with an iceberg, the tragedy became fodder for the grist mills of Hearst's pulp empire as newspapers explored every facet of the *Titanic* demise and the more than 1500 souls who perished.

The story got off to a tepid start as the men in the wireless room on the *Titanic* who first telegraphed to Cape Race the news that the ship had hit an iceberg, even admitted later to having made light of the possibility that the ship would sink.

Within ten minutes the seriousness of the sinking ship sunk in to Harold Bride and Jack Phillips, who lost his life as he used every minute to transmit calls for help. Bride later told the investigating enquiry in England that he last saw Phillips as he ran aft following his release from his duties by the Captain.

The first reports came from the *Titanic* which sent out their urgent messages to Cape Race and to other ships.

Ironically, the wireless equipment had been malfunctioning on the *Titanic* on April 14th. After the equipment was restored to working order, the backlog of messages, for which the White Star Line made handsome sums, was keeping the wireless operators busy. When a message came in from the Californian, letting them know that the ship had found so much ice that the captain ordered the ship to pause for the night, the telegraph operator was met with a rude response.

"Shut up, we are busy sending telegrams" was the response from the *Titanic*. At that point, the *Californian*, just 30 miles away, shut off her telegraph and the operator went to sleep.

In the news business, both in 1912 as well as in 2012, it takes two to tango.

On April 14, 1912, the closest party able to receive a desperate plea for help, the *Californian* wireless operator, was asleep. That situation would later change as a result of the inquiries held by both the United States and Britain and safety standards adopted included a requirement that all ships keep a telegraph operator on duty 24 hours.

The first responders of the sea began to rush towards the Titanic to save her passengers and crew. The message had become increasingly desperate. "We are sinking by the head," said the message from the Titanic. In sharp contrast to the first messages pleading for help from the Titanic, were the silly conditions on the Concordia. In the 2012 *Concordia* capsizing, Italian Coast Guard officials called the ship and offered aid and assistance, telling the ship that passengers were calling ashore and reporting that they were sinking and had been ordered to lifeboat stations. The incredible response was that all was well on the ship that they simply had experienced a "blackout".

In spite of the most advanced and modern technology available to the Concordia, the common thread in both disasters was the human element.

On the *Titanic,* Capt. Smith had ignored at least six warnings during the day of icebergs and in the fifteen minutes prior to Titanic striking the iceberg, the lookouts had sent three warnings to the bridge of looming icebergs.

The silly antics of the *Concordia* captain have made him the butt of wry jokes, which, were it not for his actions costing the lives of 32 passengers and crew, might be funny.

For the *Titanic* disaster, even before the ship sank, the first news reports began to circle the globe due to the wireless telegraph reports to newspaper offices around the world. There was a glaring error made during the process. A garbled message began with the question: "are all saved". The reply came back in error and was retransmitted: "all saved".

Within hours presses were rolling in London, New York and Washington, D.C., as well as across the continents.

The early news reports began to build fantasy on error and reports were carried in banner headlines on front pages that the *Titanic* was "Under Tow to Halifax".

The New York World reported the "**liner takes off passengers; Titanic said to be sinking**". The same front page on April 15th, reported the ship to be under tow. By the time the newspaper was reporting that news, the *Titanic* had reached its final destination at the bottom of the sea, about two miles from the surface.

The New York World wasn't the only newspaper to run with the errors mixed with the conjured and fabricated news stories.

The Washington Post reported in a banner headline which reached the full width of its front page: "**Titanic's 1,470 Passengers Are Now Being Transferred in Lifeboats to Cunard Liner**".

The Christian Science Monitor also ran with the story that all passengers were safe and had been transferred to another ship while the Titanic was under tow.

An English newspaper reported that the Titanic would have to be towed back to Britain as there were no shipyards in America large enough to work on the Titanic.

The *New York World* printed even more details about the Titanic, reporting that the ship's bow had been "**Crumpled by Collision with Iceberg**".

Not only witness testimony by the crew at the official inquiries on both sides of the Atlantic revealed that the ship had not hit the iceberg head-on but had brushed by it on the starboard side with an underwater protrusion ripping open the hull like a can opener.

The New York World staff must have been in a real frenzy conjuring up more details. The newspaper reported that the Allan Liner *Virginian* was towing the *Titanic*, which was in 'bad shape' to Halifax.

The many notable passengers were reported by the *New York World* to have been transferred from the *Titanic* to the *Carpathia* and the *Parisian*. In reality, the *Carpathia* actually did pick up all of the survivors while the *Parisian* didn't find anyone alive.

The London Daily Mail also reported in early coverage that "**NO LIVES LOST. COLLISION WITH AN ICEBERG. 2,358 LIVES IN PERIL. RUSH OF LINERS TO THE RESCUE. ALL PASSENGERS TAKEN OFF**".

SPHERE

low the Steamer Routes Cut Through Fog and Ice.

Chapter Two – Big Errors

The initial news coverage of the *Titanic* crash into an iceberg was mostly in error due to misunderstandings. In addition to the honest errors the truth of the disaster took tragic departures when considering the horror facing the families on both sides of the Atlantic who were dreading the fate of their loved ones.

False hope soon gave way to tearful waiting in Ireland, France, England and the United States. Many immigrants were also on board from dozens of other nations including Italy, Syria, Germany and Netherlands. Many of the crew was from Southampton and Liverpool and family members gathered outside White Star Line offices awaiting word of the survivors which had been picked up early on the morning of April 15, 1912.

What was the motivation for reporters and editors who were formulating the front pages of many newspapers to report news stories which were not true? Did they not know the truth?

Hindsight is always excellent vision and the rush to compete with the latest edition of the *Titanic* story must have been overwhelming. While it might be charitable to give those who put out blatantly wrong information, a free pass, history deserves an accurate account.

The Titanic Historical Society and the International Titanic Society are two of the resources available to the reader to learn about the many inaccuracies of the stories about the *RMS Titanic* sinking.

Libraries in Washington, New York, Belfast, Richmond, Halifax and London are just a few with extensive Titanic collections of news coverage of the event.

Those unfamiliar with the process of collecting raw news, verifying the information, checking the facts and preparing the news for final publication can be quick to brand honest errors as "yellow journalism" or tabloid news. The academics that sit in back in their chairs decades later and prepare lesson plans for their students have been quick to simply brand the inaccuracies as "yellow journalism". That kind of narrow-minded teacher does their students no favor.

Certainly the efforts by William Randolph Hearst newspapers to slam-dunk Bruce Ismay and brand him as "Brute Ismay" were a tabloid tactic designed to sell papers. The headlines were also an attempt to pepper a 'villain' with the disdain of the nation, whether he deserved it or not. Then there were the honest errors usually associated with a failure to fact check before laying the type on newsprint.

It is important to sort out the differences between intentional sensationalism and honest errors.

108   THE SPHERE   [May 4, 1912

Icebergs and the "Titanic":

The Size and Shape of North Atlantic Bergs.

A NORTH ATLANTIC BERG SHOWING PROJECTING SHELF AND CRACK

On the extreme right the long flat projecting arm of shelf probably extends under water for some distance further. It is on some such shelf that it is believed the "Titanic" struck. The arrow indicates the position of a large crack. One member of the "Titanic's" crew states that there was "a lot of ice" on the liner's deck. A man who saw men running up to some passengers with a piece of ice in his hand saying: "Still you believe it now?" Had such a mass as is here shown been inserted in the vessel's contact the people might have been all more careless and doubtless.

Portion of Iceberg Falling into the Sea.

This view was obtained in the North Atlantic at the very moment when a large piece of ice toal some ico point upon it was falling into the water

A LARGE BERG WITH A STEAMER IN CLOSE PROXIMITY—AT ST. JOHN'S, NEWFOUNDLAND

The above direct photographic view gives a good idea of the size and shape of North Atlantic icebergs. A recent witness at the American inquiry states that the height of the fatal berg was 60 ft. Between 70 ft. and 100 ft. were the dimensions given in last week's "Sphere." There is a tendency to believe that the dimensions of the berg were even less but instances have been mentioned, but there is no doubt, on the other hand that a height of 60 ft. does not concede a very large berg (see dimensions given in amount above)

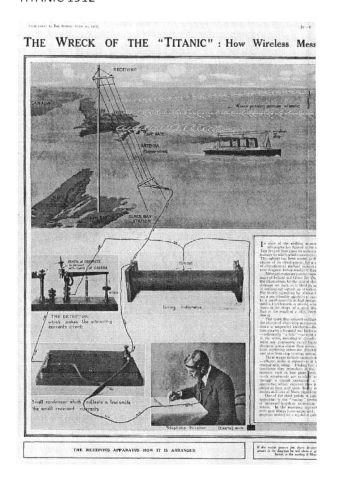

THE WRECK OF THE "TITANIC" : How Wireless Mess

THE RECEIVING APPARATUS HOW IT IS ARRANGED

Chapter Three – Wireless News

Scene one of the lead-ins to the sinking of the *Titanic* has to be that fateful room where telegraph operators Jack Phillips and Harold Bride worked at processing the huge backlog of messages which came in to the Titanic on April 14, 1912.

Included in the volume of messages were important weather reports that came from other ships and that the two had to relay on to Cape Race, Newfoundland. Those messages dealt with ice fields in the path of the *Titanic*.

While some report that the operators simply sent the messages on to Cape Race, other witnesses were quoted in news reports as well as in Logan Marshall's survivor accounts, that Capt. Smith received such reports and simply stuffed them in his pocket.

As the scene of the world's biggest news story shifted to night, the reports from the lookouts to the bridge of ice bergs ahead were ignored until it was too late. Frederick Fleet would later testify that he did not have binoculars as the previous crew left the ship in Ireland and took the lookout binoculars with them.

Even without the binoculars, the lookouts spotted the iceberg and gave three warnings, all of which were ignored.

Again, the tragic scene shifts to the telegraph room where minutes after the iceberg opened up the hull of the ship like it was a can-opener, Phillips and Bride were instructed to send messages pleading for assistance.

There is ample evidence that the message for C. Q. D. (Come Quickly, Danger) and S.O.S. were indeed understood.

Captain Arthur Rostron of the *Carpathia* did just about everything right that a captain could do in an emergency. His actions were well chronicled and reported in the newspapers along with the accounts of the accolades and thanks of the survivors which were heaped upon him.

The *Carpathia* quickly turned in its tracks and began to race towards the coordinates sent by the Titanic.

Capt. Rostron ordered that the steam heat to the passenger cabins on the *Carpathia* be turned off so that all of the available steam was used for the ship's engines to speed her on the way to the rescue. He ordered double lookouts so that his ship did not meet the same fate as the *Titanic.* He also ordered hot cocoa, tea and coffee brewed along with large quantities of soup to warm survivors.

The news coverage of the Titanic disaster changed from the scene inside the telegraph room on the Titanic to the receiving radio transmitters on ships and land stations around the world.

One of the first to receive the news of the Titanic sinking was a young man who worked for Marconi Company in a radio signal station on the top floor of the Wannamaker's Department Store in New York City. He was 21 year-old David Sarnoff, who went on to create the first national radio network of NBC, which later also became the first television network.

But the biggest blunders of the first night of the reporting of the *Titanic* sinking were that "all were saved" and that the ship was under tow to Halifax".

While it is understandable how the confused message mixed up the story of the survivors, it is clear that inventive reporting concocted the story that the ship "was under tow". The *Titanic* arrived on the sea bottom at about 2:30 am, Monday, April 15th, about the same time that many newspapers around the world were telling their readers that the crippled ship was slowly proceeding towards Halifax, Nova Scotia.

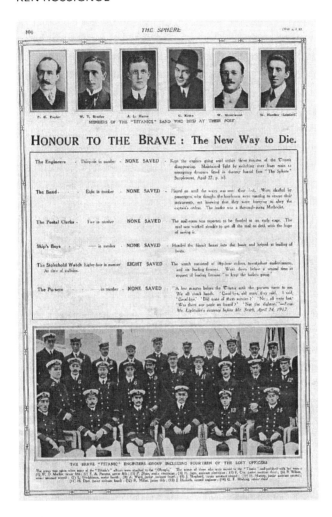

Chapter Four – All Saved

One can imagine the chaos inside the newsrooms of the world's leading newspapers as they soon learned that they had gotten the story so badly wrong, as to "**ALL SAVED**". Compounded to that error were the elaborate accounts of the ship being crippled and being towed to Canada by *The Virginian.*

With so many newspapers being completely bamboozled by the confusion and the fabrication involved in the first day of news reporting, the facts of the rescue began to drip out from the telegraph room of the *Carpathia.*

In fact, it took seventeen hours before the correct facts of the *Titanic* disaster to come out.

On board the rescue ship was the assistant telegraph operator of the *Titanic* - Harold Bride. Bride's own story of survival was authentic and inspiring and he surely deserved to be able to sell his story and he did. The *New York Times* paid $500 for his story in a great example of "checkbook journalism" that would make the politically correct *New York Times* staff of today blush with embarrassment.

Bride told the investigating committee in New York that he sent his last message for help as the ship was sinking and he ran for the aft where a group of men were trying to get a boat loose which had been stuck on the deck. At that point a large wave knocked the boat loose and as he had a grip on an oarlock, he went with it. He soon found himself holding onto an overturned boat and pulled himself up on the boat's bottom. A man was lying atop of his legs which were pushed down into the slats of the bottom of the boat. Soon the *Titanic* slipped out of sight even with the band delivering their final rendition of "Autumn". Bride told of "some splendid people saved us. They had a right-side up boat and it was full to capacity. Yet they came to us and loaded us all into it. I saw some lights off in the distance and knew a steamship was coming to our aid."

Bride also told of the heroics of Jack Phillips, who kept sending telegraph messages of their condition and location to other ships long after the Captain released him from duty. Bride spoke of the actions of Phillips and the dedication of the band as "two things that stand out in my mind over all the rest".

When Bride was brought aboard the *Carpathia*, he was suffering from frostbite on his crippled feet and yet he was given warm clothes and he went right to work sending telegrams.

The newsrooms in the fiercely competitive offices of the *New York Times, New York World, New York Herald, New York Tribune* and other newspaper offices across America and around the world were in turmoil.

According to preserved front pages of many newspapers, their news accounts began to recover from the errors of the first day and slowly the facts began to be presented accurately.

The Baltimore American reported on Tuesday, April 16, 1912 that 1600 died while "**866 Women and Children Saved**". While both figures were incorrect, they weren't off by that much with slightly more than 1500 perished and about 705 saved. Most striking was the front page listing of the names of those who were rescued. The fact that the *Carpathia* was still at sea and the *Titanic* had been at the bottom for about 24 hours and the *Baltimore American* still had the listing of the names of those saved was amazing. A major metropolitan newspaper or television station would be hard put to do any better today, one hundred years later.

TITANIC 1912

17

Chapter Five

- Senator's Tirade against Ismay

Amazingly, a U. S. Senate investigating committee arrived in New York City just two days after the survivors were brought to shore on the *Carpathia*. At least four

Senators, including Sen. Isidor Rayner of Maryland and of Sen. William Alden Smith, of Michigan, the chairman of the sub-committee on the Senate Committee on Commerce, were on the scene at the East Room of the Waldorf-Astoria Hotel in New York.

The committee convened on the first day after the *Carpathia* docked and immediately began taking testimony with fiery blasts at White Star Managing Director Bruce Ismay, who survived the sinking of his ship.

According to the front page coverage of *The World*, Sen. Rayner blasted Ismay for being one of the survivors and for his orders to Capt. Smith to race across the ocean in a zeal for record-setting.

Ismay was cool in his responses and noted that while the ship had made good time, that one boiler was never lit off and used during the voyage and that setting a speed record was not a goal.

In fact, it was clear from many available witnesses interviewed in news accounts that there was no point in the *Titanic* arriving in New York earlier than planned.

Just as in modern travel, the passengers of the *Titanic* had hotel rooms and trains booked and an arrival a day early would have caused havoc to their arrangements.

Sen. Rayner railed against Ismay nonetheless; a case of grandstanding that would make today's U. S. Senators jealous with envy.

"He risked the lives of the entire ship to make a speedy passage across the sea," said Sen. Rayner in what *The World* called a "bitter attack".

The newspaper reported Sen. Rayner as saying that Ismay should be "held responsible for the disaster and that civilized nations would applaud criminal prosecution of management of the line".

Ismay held firm in his contention that he had never issued any orders to Capt. Smith and there is no evidence that a senior captain of the fleet would have cared should Ismay had interfered with the navigational duties of the ship's master. Capt. Smith was set to retire after the maiden voyage of the *Titanic* was unlikely to have paid any heed to Ismay.

Ismay said there was no reason to hurry across the sea and that the engines were not making full speed, even though he admitted it had been making 21 knots.

After the lambasting of Ismay by the stinging words of the Senator from Maryland, the attention turned to the matter-of-fact testimony of Capt. Arthur Henry Rostron and his rush across the waves to reach the Titanic.

Rostron told of his daring race at 17 knots, the fastest ever for his older Cunard liner.

The World headlined his story with another banner headline: "**CARPATHIA DODGED 20 BERGS IN WILD DASH TO SAVE TITANIC**"

The same senator who wanted to hang the owner of the *Titanic* for its ship traveling at breakneck speed through the ice field sat by quietly while the captain of the Carpathia told of his rescue effort at a mere four knots slower speed.

Capt. Rostron told of the recovery of the survivors and the burial service he held over what he believed to be the grave of the RMS Titanic and more than 1500 souls. The newspaper said that those in the room were moved to tears at the captain's words.

One other decision of Capt. Rostron was to limit the use of the Marconi telegraph to sending the names of the survivors and to confirm that others from the Titanic were not on the ship and presumed dead. He banned communication with the newspapers.

At one point, the White House communicated a question from the President as to the status of his aide, Maj. Archibald Butt. Maj. Butt, Col. Astor and others of the wealthy and powerful on the ship had shepherded the loading of the women and children and then went down with the ship.

First newspaper reports included the news that the President was turned down in his request to learn about Maj. Butt. Testimony later at the hearing denied that claim and said that the President's inquiry was answered simply that "Maj. Butt is not here on the Carpathia."

Chapter Six - Louis & Lola

A Frenchman abducted his two sons from their mother and using an assumed name, booked passage at Cherbourg, France, on the Titanic. Michel Navratil, using the assumed name, Louis Hoffman, boarded with his two sons, Michel and Edmond, ages four and two, were off to America.

On the eventful night of tragedy, Michel carefully dressed his two sons and placed them in the hands of the Second Officer Charles Lightoller who was in command of loading the last collapsible life raft to leave the sinking ship.

The news reports called the pair the "Waifs of the Titanic" and "Orphans of the Deep".

A headline in The World declared "FATHER TOSSSED HIS BABIES FROM TITANIC TO LIFEBOAT".

The news account explains how the father rushed to the side of the ship and first dropped the older boy into the arms of a sailor and then the second one. Regardless of the dramatic delivery of the two accounts, given the desperate situation for the various witnesses, anything close to either account is believable.

Photos of the two children were circulated by newspapers in North America and in Europe. Soon the boy's mother recognized them back in Nice. Marcelle Navratil was soon on her way to claim her children and the White Star Line paid her passage to New York to retrieve her sons.

The oldest child, Michel, lived to the age of 92 and died in 2001. Michel always told anyone who would listen that he died at age four. "Since then I have always been a fare-dodger of life. A gleaner of time."

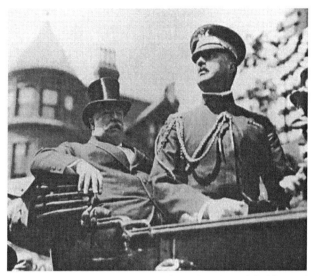

President William Howard Taft, left, with Maj. Archibald Butt, his chief of staff.

Chapter Seven – Maj. Archibald Butt

Also appearing on April 17, 1912 was a front page headline in the *Los Angeles Times*: "**MAJ. BUTT, WITH GUN IN HAND, HELD BACK FRENZIED MEN, SAVED WOMEN, and CAPT. SMITH A SUICIDE**".
Maj. Archibald Butt, 41, was a resident of Washington, D.C. and had been a correspondent for a number of Southern newspapers prior to his Army service in the Spanish American War.

Butt had been sent to Italy by President William Howard Taft to take a message to the Pope and to Italian King Victor Emmanuel.

The New York Times reported that Butt had been one of the more popular figures in Washington society but it was a role in supervising a shipload of mules that caught the attention of the President.

Butt had been commissioned as a Captain in the Quartermaster's Department of the Army and was to be detailed to Manila on the transport Sumner and to travel by way of the Suez Canal.

Butt was able to get his travel orders changed to the Dix leaving from San Francisco with a cargo of 500 mules and instructions to see to it that they were given a rest at Honolulu. When Butt learned what the charges would be at Hawaii, he refused to allow the exorbitant charges to be placed and kept the mules on the ship for the trip to the Philippines.

The animals were well-tended on the voyage and made it to Manila in good health, which was lucky for Butt as he would have been court-martialed had harm had come to them.

After writing several articles about the care of animals in the tropics, Butt caught the attention of President Theodore Roosevelt. Roosevelt appointed Butt his top aide, an equivalent position today as the Chief of Staff. After Roosevelt left office, Butt retained the post under Taft and both men grew to have high esteem for each other.

The background in news coverage in the days following the disaster involving Maj. Butt was superficial in nature due to his high position.

However more about him was gleaned from his own letters which were saved and later donated to a library which told a lot about the details of his life in Washington.

In one letter to his mother, Butt noted that he had been assigned the task to tell a diplomat and the wife of a high-ranking official to end their affair. Another incident calling on his expertise had to do with the removal of a couch from the White House. He also told of his need to acquire a gun to take on outings with the President. A letter also discussed the personality of Mrs. Roosevelt.

One incident of note was when an administration official allowed the White House grounds to be loaned to The Society of Fallen Women.

Butt also noted in a private letter that he had let the President of Harvard know that he felt that the college was not appropriate for southern boys due to the "intellectual snobbery" of the college.

The news coverage of the heroism of Maj. Butt and Col. Astor was consistent: "**MAJOR BUTT AND COLONEL ASTOR TOGETHER AS STEAMER SUNK**" proclaimed the Los Angeles Times.

The New York Tribune reported: Mrs. Straus Refused to Leave Her Husband; Major Butt and Colonel Astor Together as Steamer Sank

MEN IN 1ST AND 2ND CABINS CALM; ITALIANS SHOT TO KEEP ORDER

The Tribune continued the banner headline coverage blaming the disaster on the speed of the liner, in fact, said it was "speeding".

Dr. Washington Dodge, of San Francisco was in the Hotel Wolcott in New York when he gave an interview which appeared in *The Bulletin* newspaper in San Francisco on April 19, 1912. Dodge told awakening after the collision with the ice berg and soon of the launching of the lifeboats.

"As the lifeboats were being launched, many of the first-class passengers expressed their preference for staying on the ship. The passengers were constantly being assured that there was no danger, but that as a matter of extra precaution the women and children should be placed in the lifeboats."

"Everything was quiet and orderly and I placed Mrs. Dodge and the boy in the fourth or fifth boat. I believe there were 20 boats lowered away altogether. I did what I could to help in keeping order, as after the sixth or seventh boat was launched the excitement began."

"Some of the passengers fought with such desperation to get into the lifeboats that the officers shot them, and their bodies fell into the ocean."

"It was 10:30 pm when the collision occurred, and at 1:55 o'clock when the ship went down," he said. "Major Archibald Butt stood with John Jacob Astor as the water rolled over the *Titanic*."

Dodge told of a steward grabbing him pushing him into a boat full with women and children, exclaiming that he needed his help in caring for his charges.

When the lifeboat pulled away, Dodge said he could hear the band playing "Lead, Kindly Light" and rockets going up into the clear night.

"We could see from the distance that two boats were being made ready to be lowered. The panic was in the steerage, and it was in that portion of the ship that the shooting was made necessary."

"I will never forget," Mrs. Dodge said, "the awful scene of the great steamer as we drew away. From the upper rails heroic husbands and fathers were waving and throwing kisses to their womenfolk in the receding lifeboats."

President's Aide Had Gone on a Special Mission to the Pope

Special to *The New York Times*

WASHINGTON, April 15.-Major Archibald Willingham

Butt, President Taft's Military Aide, was returning on the Titanic after a visit to Rome, where he went to see the Pope and King Victor Emmanuel. He undoubtedly went there as a personal messenger from the President. He is supposed to have been bearing home to President Taft an important message from the Pope.

Major Butt has been one of the most popular officers in the army. He was born in Georgia forty-one years ago. For several years before the Spanish war he was a newspaper correspondent in Washington, representing at one time *The Louisville Post, The Atlanta Constitution, The Nashville Banner, The Augusta Chronicle, and The Savannah News.* From his first arrival in Washington he has been popular in society.

He accepted the position of First Secretary of the United States Legation at the City of Mexico when former Senator Matt Y. Ransom of North Carolina was Minister, and remained there until the death of Ransom, when he returned to newspaper work in Washington. One of his diversions during his years of work as a newspaper writer was to write for magazines, and he produced several novels based on his life in Mexico and the South that rose to a more than ordinary level of finish and interest.

His entry in the army was due to the late Major Gen. H. C. Corbin, who was Adjutant General during the Spanish War and the years following, and who selected Butt as one of twenty young officers to go into the fifteen new volunteer regiments to go to the Philippines.

He was commissioned a Captain in the Quartermaster's Department and was slated to go to Manila on the transport Sumner by way of Suez. With great difficulty he got the order changed and went on the Dix from San Francisco with a cargo of 500 mules. His orders told him to unload the mules at Honolulu and give them a rest, but the young officer found the charges for feed and stables so high there he contented himself with swearing at the Hawaiians and kept every mule on ship and went on. He would have been court-martialed if any of them had died, but he landed them all safe and well, and, in fact, better than when they came on board.

While in the Islands he wrote several reports on handling animals in the tropics that attracted attention and one of his military articles so pleased President Roosevelt that he later asked him to become his military aide. On his return from the Philippines Butt was given a commission in the regular army and sent to Cuba with the Army of Occupation. He was stationed at Havana and did very good service there. Within a month after his return to duly in the Quartermaster's Department, President Roosevelt had him detailed to duty as one of his personal aides.

Butt kept up with Roosevelt in all his physical stunts, made the famous ride to Warrenton and back in one afternoon, climbed the heights of Rock Creek Canyon with the President and Prince Henry, and at the same time reduced the handling of crowds at the White House receptions to a fine art. He made the record there of remembering the names and introducing 1,280 persons in one hour. Major Butt was an ideal clubman, for he knew everyone and was liked by all. While in Manila he was Secretary of the Army and Navy Club there.

He was a bachelor and lived in a fine old mansion here where he entertained his old friends in handsome style. His name was several times mentioned in rumors of his engagement to some of the prettiest and most popular young women in society, but one of the last things he did just before sailing for Rome was to deny in a jocular way a report that he was finally engaged and remarked that he had been a bachelor so long that he thought he had better stay so to the end of the chapter.

Throughout Washington to-night every comment on the disaster is followed by the expression, "I hope Butt is safe." Major Butt was a graduate of Sewanee University, Tennessee. He was promoted to the grade a year ago after an eleven years' record of most excellent service. He had a brother living in London, where his mother died a few years ago.

Statement by President Taft on death of Maj. Butt:

After finding that Butt's name was not on the list of survivors, Taft replied, "I never had any idea that Archie was saved at all. As soon as I heard that 1200 people went down I knew he went down too. He was a soldier and was on deck where he belonged. I know Archie died like a soldier."

ADRIFT IN AN OPEN BOAT

San Francisco Examiner — April 19, 1912.

Chapter Eight – Titanic was on fire!

On Friday, April 19th, the *Richmond Times Dispatch* joined a growing number of American newspapers that began to report accurately as to the numbers of lives lost as well as saved. The death toll in a large banner front page was set as 1601 and 739 listed as survived. The newspaper reported that six persons were buried at sea as they died on the Carpathia after being rescued.

By the next day, the second days of Senate committee hearings were being reported.

The World carried a banner headline: "**FALSE TITANIC REPORTS NOT FROM CARPATHIA".**

"I sent no message that she was in tow" was a bold sub headline on the lead story of the day. The statement was attributed to Harold Bride, the assistant Marconi operator on the Titanic that had gone to work on the Carpathia as soon as he was rescued. "**I REMAINED ON DUTY FOR 3 FULL DAYS**" proclaimed another bold headline.

At the hearing, Bride told the senators that the first report of ice bergs had come at 4 pm Sunday. But Bride and H. T. Cottam, the Carpathia operator both strongly denied sending any messages from the Carpathia that implied or construed in any fashion the news that the Titanic was under tow to Halifax.

Cottam told the Senate panel that the first message he had from the Titanic was from Jack Phillips and said: "Come at once, C. D.Q., old man". "Come as quickly as possible. She's taking water and it's up to the boilers."

"I never heard from her after that," said Cottam. "Although several times I called the Titanic and sent Capt. Rostron's reply to Phillip's last message which read: "We are making your position as quickly as possible. Have double watch in the engine room. We are making 15 to 16 knots an hour. Get your boats ready. We have ours ready."

The *Carpathia* arrived on the scene at about 4:30 am and by 6 am had taken all aboard from the lifeboats.

The front page of *The World* on Saturday, April 20th dealt primarily with the Senate hearing and the effort to learn how the false reports of everyone saved and the ship being under tow came about.

But the most shocking news was the first report that the *Titanic* had been on fire.

"FIRE IN TITANIC'S HOLD RAGED UNABATED 5 DAYS"

The White Star Liner *Titanic* was on fire from the day she sailed from Southampton. Her officers and crew knew it, for they had fought the fire for days.

This story, told the first time today by the survivors of the crew who were sent back to England on board the liner Lapland, was only one of the many thrilling tales of the first – and the last- voyage of the Titanic.

"The *Titanic* sailed from Southampton on Wednesday, April 10 at noon," said J. Dilley, fireman on the Titanic. "I was assigned to the Titanic from the Oceanic where I had served as a fireman. From the day we sailed, the Titanic was on fire and my sole duty, together with eleven other men, had been to fight that fire. We had made no headway against it.

"Of course, sir," he went on, "the passengers knew nothing of the fire. Do you think, sir, we'd have let them know about it? No sir. The fire started in bunker No. 6. There were hundreds of tons of coal stored there. The coal on top of the bunker was wet but down at the bottom of the bunker the coal had been permitted to get dry."

The dry coal at the bottom of the pile took fire, sir, and smoldered for days. The wet coal on top kept the flames from coming through, but down in the bottom of the bunker, sir, the flames were raging."

"Two men from each watch of stokers was tolled off, sir, to fight that fire. The stokers, you know, sir, work four hours at a time, so twelve of us was fighting flames from the day we put out of Southampton until we hit the damned iceberg."

"No sir, we didn't get that fire out, and among the stokers there was talk sir, that we'd have to empty the big coal bunkers after we put our passengers off in New York, and then call on the fireboats there to help us put out the fire."

"But we didn't need such help. It was right under Bunker No. 6 that the iceberg tore the biggest hole in the Titanic and the flood of water that came through, sir, put out the fire that our tons and tons of water hadn't been able to get rid of."

"The stokers were beginning to get alarmed over it but the officers told us to keep our mouths shut – they didn't want to alarm the passengers."

Noted *Titanic* author and editor Bruce M. Caplan provided this information for this book as to the fire in the Titanic coal bunkers:

"I think this is the real reason the iceberg was able to penetrate the steel!" said Caplan, who was kind enough to provide this transcript of the British hearing.

Testimony at British Enquiry---Charles Hendrickson

Day Five--

5232. Do you remember a fire in a coal bunker on board this boat?
- Yes.
5233. Is it a common occurrence for fires to take place on boats?
- No.
5234. It is not common?
- No.

5235. How long have you been on a White Star boat?

- About five years.

5236. When did you last see a fire in a coal bunker?

- I never saw one before.

5237. It has been suggested that fires in coal bunkers are quite a common occurrence, but you have been five years in the White Star line and have not seen a fire in a coal bunker?

- No.

5238. Did you help to get the coal out?

- Yes.

5239. Did you hear when the fire commenced?

- Yes, I heard it commenced at Belfast.

5240. When did you start getting the coal out?

- The first watch we did from Southampton we started to get it out.

5241. How many days would that be after you left Belfast?

- I do not know when she left Belfast to the day.

5242. It would be two or three days, I suppose?

- I should say so.

5243. Did it take much time to get the fire down?

- It took us right up to the Saturday to get it out.

5244. How long did it take to put the fire itself out?

- The fire was not out much before all the coal was out.

5245. The fire was not extinguished until you got the whole of the coal out?

- No. I finished the bunker out myself, me and three or four men that were there. We worked everything out.

5246. The bulkhead forms part of the bunker - the side?

- Yes, you could see where the bulkhead had been red hot.

5247. You looked at the side after the coal had been taken out?

- Yes.

5248. What condition was it in?
- You could see where it had been red hot; all the paint and everything was off. It was dented a bit.
   5249. It was damaged, at any rate?
- Yes, warped.
   5250. Was much notice taken of it? Was any attempt made to do anything with it?
- I just brushed it off and got some black oil and rubbed over it.
   5251. To give it its ordinary appearance?
Yes.

As to the subject of "brittle steel", this information from Caplan pertains to the condition of the hull in the area of the fire, as well as the entire hull:

In the mid-90s Tom McCluskie, Administration Manager, Harland & Wolff, Technical Services Ltd. in Belfast, Northern Ireland commented on the quality of steel used with Titanic: Titanic, as with all ships built for the White Star Line by Harland & Wolff was built on a "cost-plus" basis; the finest materials available were used in construction since they had no limitations on their budget. Other ships built at that time were manufactured with the same steel. Her sister Olympic that collided with the cruiser Hawke on September 11, 1911 (see images of damage) proved the strength of her shell plates. Not only that accident but during the First World War, she ran over and sank an enemy submarine and near the end of her career rammed the Nantucket lightship, sinking it. Olympic was built in 1910-11, lived to a ripe old age when she was finally scrapped in 1936. Brittle steel? Hardly.

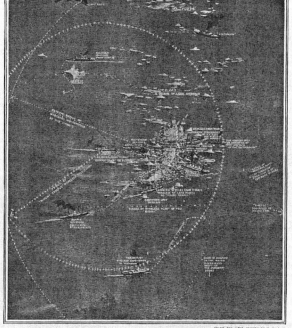

Ships which Might have Rescued Everyone on the "Titanic" if Events had only Been a Little Different.

THE APPROXIMATE POSITIONS OF NEIGHBOURING SHIPS AT THE TIME OF THE "TITANIC" DISASTER

Chapter Nine- 'Titanic in Tow' Denials

The hot potato at the Senate hearings in New York continued to try to cast blame on someone for the false reports of the saving of all those on the stricken ship as well as the claim that the ship was under tow.

The World on April 20th carried a front page story from Plymouth, England that quoted the captain of the *Olympic* at denying that his ship had sent the erroneous messages.

"Captain Haddock of the *Olympic* today positively and emphatically denied that he wireless message which the operator at the Cape Race station says was picked up by him, saying that the *Virginian* was towing the Titanic, was sent from his vessel."

"I never had any information to that effect," said Capt. Haddock, "and the intimation that it was sent by me to the Cape Race man is absolute injustice. I do not know from whom he could have received that message."

The story that I sent it is a flagrant invention. As soon as I heard of the disaster from the *Carpathia* I dispatched the news by wireless to New York. That was on Monday afternoon."

"The *Olympic*" the captain continued, "first heard the Titanic's call for aid about twenty minutes after the mishap had occurred. It came through the steamer "*Celtic*" and we never heard direct from Capt. Smith. Five hundred miles separated the *Olympic* and *Titanic* and utilizing every pound of steam, the Olympic pressed forward at a pace never before steamed by her- between 24 and 25 knots per hour."

"Hours later the *Olympic* knew that her race to the Titanic had been in vain. The Carpathia announced that she had the survivors aboard and that the Titanic had disappeared. Gloom settled over the Olympic and all amusements were abandoned.

A committee formed under the chairmanship of Albert Wiggin collected $7,000 for the relief of the sufferers.

The wireless operators and passengers on board the *Olympic* were bombarded with requests for stories of disaster but censorship was established over the wireless service so as to shut off the possibility of groundless rumors being circulated."

Other details brought out by survivors at the Senate hearing brought more to light of the fateful voyage.

"The horrors of the disaster grew very real before the committee when Harold S. Bride, the extra wireless operator of the *Titanic,* took the stand. Bride, a pale-faced black haired boy of eighteen, was carried into the room. Both of his feet, frozen in the terrible hours between the time he left the sinking *Titanic* and the time he reached the *Carpathia*, were swathed in heavy bandages. His face was drawn with pain and his big black eyes were red and sunken.

While Bride was testifying several newspaper photographers exploded flashbulbs. The report startled everyone in the room and Bride's shattered nerves almost gave way.

Yesterday's session lasted from forenoon until almost midnight. Its chief feature was the first official statement of the catastrophe- that of Second Officer Charles Lightoller, the senior officer surviving of the *Titanic.*

"One of the things already brought out at the Investigation is that at least 198 persons died needlessly on the Titanic because in six lifeboats that would have easily carried 390 persons, only 192 persons were sent away. These boats were all that went on one side of the ship."

"The Committee began today to go into details of the disaster from various angles. At yesterday's session, J. Bruce Ismay told why he was on the Titanic and how he got off. Capt. Rostron of the *Carpathia* told how he rescued the Titanic survivors, and Marconi, the wireless man, told the workings of the wireless system at sea."

"Second Officer Lightoller told a long and clear story of the part he played in the wreck at last night's session of the committee. He had a remarkable experience in that he went down with the vessel, was twice sucked under and twice blown to the surface by an explosion in the hull of the ship."

Chapter Ten – No Woman Shall Die Here Because I am a Coward

That Benjamin Guggenheim, who went down with the *Titanic*, died as bravely as the best, was definitely made known today through a message the young multimillionaire sent his wife by his room steward on the doomed ship. The steward, Johnson, was tolled off to one of the lifeboats. Johnson called at the St. Regis and delivered his message.

"Tell my wife, if I don't get away, that I could not leave the ship until all the women were safe. No woman shall go to the bottom because I was a coward. Tell her my last thoughts will be of her."

Those were the words the steward brought ashore as Guggenheim's last message. This information was given by Daniel Guggenheim, eldest of the seven-now six-brothers, world famous as millionaire mining men.

According to Johnson, Guggenheim was in his stateroom just after the crash and Johnson helped him dress. Guggenheim was calm, as was his secretary Guglio. After dressing, he went on deck with Guglio. Johnson was ordered to his post at one of the lifeboats. He urged Guggenheim to try to get into a boat in which they were taking some men.

"It is not my place to take a boat yet," said the young millionaire. "There are seems to be a man's work to do yet on this ship. If there are boats for all the women, I'll try to get away."

Then he gave Johnson the message for Mrs. Guggenheim, shook hands with the steward and walked away with Guglio.

Chapter Eleven- A Change of Plans

Senator Smith was quoted in the front page story of *The World* on Saturday, April 20th with the headline: **"ISMAY'S PLAN TO FLEE WITH CREW ON *CEDRIC* HURRIED SENATE PROBE"**.

The World reported on Saturday, April 20th that a government boat had intercepted a wireless message from Ismay to General Manager Franklin of the White Star Line to stop a departing White Star liner in order that he and the surviving Titanic crew could escape America.

Sen. William Alden Smith was quoted as saying: "J. Bruce Ismay sent wireless messages to General Manager Franklin in which he urged that the outward-bound

Cedric be stopped to take himself and the crew of the Titanic aboard and back to England. These messages were picked up by the

Bruce Ismay, CEO of the White Star line.

wireless on a Government boat and Washington at once communicated with. That is why the Senate committee was so prompt in arriving in New York and why I was down on the pier when the Carpathia put in.

"Not only was Ismay eager to return to England on the Cedric, but he has been eager to get away on the Lapland since his arrival in New York. We have need of Ismay and he will remain here, for I have some more questions to ask him. The crew will also be held for a time, for many of them will be questioned."

Mr. Ismay virtually admitted

U. S. Senate Commerce Committee hearing held at the Waldorf Astoria in New York.

sending the messages in question today. He was questioned about the matter before the session of the Senatorial Investigating Committee.

"The facts speak for themselves," he said. "The only reason I am anxious to get the survivors of the crew back to England as soon as possible is because England is their home and they are anxious to get home. It would be unwise to have them loafing around New York. It is for their own interest that I am anxious to get them back to their families."

Mr. Ismay was questioned about a report that he told a Mrs. Ryerson, a passenger, on Sunday, when she spoke to him about the proximity of ice, that the *Titanic* would go faster to get past the ice. He made this comment: "Absurd".

The next day, the Red Star Liner *Lapland* cast off from New York with approximately 180 of the 206 surviving members of the *Titanic* crew. A report in *The World* revealed that the crew went as passengers in steerage and few of them wore uniforms. The majority had been furnished civilian clothing by White Star officials.

Unusual efforts were made by the Red Star line officials to prevent the *Titanic* survivors from talking, were also reported in the news account.

The moment the men were landed from the *Carpathia,* they were herded together and carried to a tug which transferred them to the Lapland, where they were quartered until sailing time today.

The Red Star line, owned by International Mercantile Marine, which also owns the White Star line, was evidently acting under orders to prevent the men from being interviewed. Permission to enter the steerage was refused, the refusal being backed up by stationing a force of men about the gangway to permit only steerage ticket holders to enter.

A large number of the *Titanic*'s sailors, however, refused to submit to the practical imprisonment and insisted on coming ashore this morning. Most of them were found in the waterfront saloons drinking beer. They were willing to talk freely.

At 9:30 am the *Titanic*'s sailors were mustered in the steerage of the Lapland and the roll called. About 150 answered present. As the men answered their names they were told that sixteen men who had been in command of the lifeboats had been ordered to remain in America to appear before the Senate Investigating Committee.

As they came from the vessel's hold, bring with them their meager belongings, several of them were in tears. One, who refused to give his name, broke away from the others and tried to re-enter the *Lapland*.

"I don't want to stay in America," he wept. I want to go back to my wife."

He was led away from the ship weeping. His fellows said he was one of the heroes of the wreck.

A GRIM TEACHER

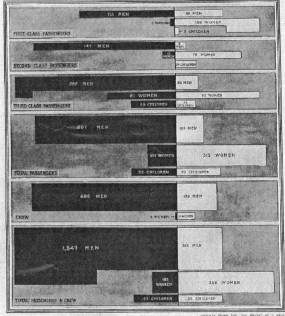

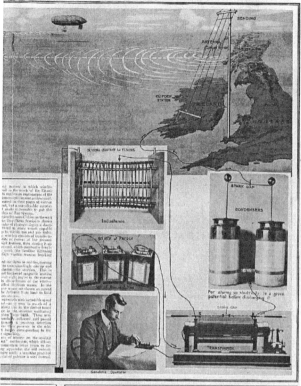

Workers pose with one of the three massive propellers of the Titanic at Harland & Wolff shipyard in Belfast.

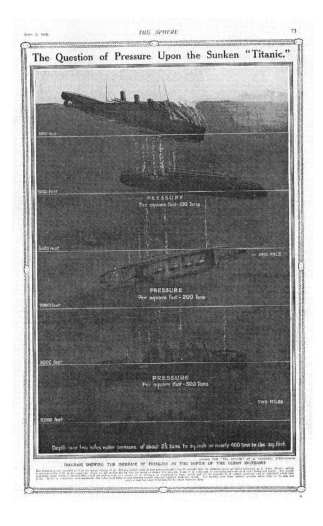

Chapter Twelve – Half a Billion!

The *Baltimore American* on the day following the sinking of the Titanic was ready to roll with the news of the wealthiest on board the doomed liner.

In a front page story, the newspaper ran an article depicted the wealthy on the ship as being worth over a half billion dollars.

John Jacob Astor heads the list, reported the paper. Benjamin Guggenheim and George Widener's fortunes also were set at "many millions". J. Bruce Ismay was reported as worth $40 million.

Untold wealth was represented among the passengers of the *Titanic*, said the breathless news report, which then set about the task of detailing the worth of those on the ship.

There were on board at least six men each of whose fortunes might be reckoned in the tens of millions of dollars. A rough estimate of the total wealth represented in the first-class passenger list would reach over a half-billion dollars.

The wealthiest of the list is Col. John Jacob Astor, head of the famous house whose name he bears, who is reputed to be worth $150,000,000. Mr. Astor was returning from a tour of Egypt with his bride, who was Miss Madeline Force, to whom he was married in Providence on Sept. 9.

Benjamin Guggenheim, probably next in financial importance, is the fifth of the seven sons of Myer Guggenheim, who founded the American Smelting and Refining Company, the great mining corporation, and is a director of many corporations, including the International Steam Pump Company, of which he is also president. His fortune is estimated at $95,000,000. His wife, whose name does not appear on the passenger list, is the daughter of James Seligman, the New York banker.

George D. Widener is the son of P. A. Widener, the Philadelphia "traction king" whose fortune is estimated at $50,000,000. Ironically, Widener was also president of a Philadelphia bank which financed much of the debt service for White Star line and its newest ship, the *RMS Titanic.*

The London Daily Graphic reported that George D. Widener had bought Rembrandt's "The Mill" for 100,000 pounds.

Isadore Straus, one of New York's most prominent dry goods merchants and a notable for his philanthropies, has a fortune also estimated to be worth $50,000,000. He is a director in various banks, trust companies and charitable institutions.

J. Bruce Ismay, president and founder of the International Mercantile Marine was on the ship and the voyage was his third on a maiden trip of a new liner owned by the firm. Ismay's worth was believed to be $40,000,000. The *Baltimore American* reported that Ismay had along with J. P. Morgan, consolidated British and American shipping lines under International Mercantile Marine control.

Another famed captain of industry was Col. Washington Roebling, the builder of the Brooklyn Bridge and president and director of John A. Roebling's Sons Company and credited with a fortune of $25,000,000.

Among others of reputed wealth who were on board the *Titanic* are: John P. Thayer, vice president of the Pennsylvania Railroad; Clarence Moore, a well-known sportsman whose wife was Miss Mabel Swift, daughter of E. C. Swift, the Chicago meatpacker, and Charles M. Hays, president of the Grand Trunk Railway of Canada.

The *London Daily Graphic* also reported that Canadian railroader Hays had once before been shipwrecked in the Pacific.

Other persons of note in the life of the arts and literature were: W. T. Stead, writer, journalist and war correspondent; Jacques Futrelle, the short story writer; Frederick M. Hoyt, a well-known New York yachtsman; Dr. Washington Dodge, of San Francisco; Henry Sleeper Harper, grandson of John Wesley Harper, one of the founders of Harper Brothers publishing house; William H. Carter, of Philadelphia and Newport, and Thomas Pears, a Pittsburgh steel manufacturer.

Christopher Head is a London barrister and son of the senior member of the firm of Lloyd's underwriters. Mrs. Edward S. Roberts is from St. Louis, as also are Miss E. W. Allen and Theophile Papin Jr. Mr. Papin is noted as an art connoisseur. Among other prominent Canadian passengers were H. Markland Molson, a banker; Mr. and Mrs. Thorston Davidson, Mrs. James Baxter, Q. Baxter, J. J. Allison and Mrs. Allison, of Montreal; Major Arthur Penchen, of the Queens Own Rifles, Toronto; Mrs. Mark Fortune and Mrs. Graham of Winnipeg.

Paul Chevre, the well-known French sculptor, who made the Champlain monument, was in the first cabin, on his way to Canada to complete the Mercier memorial. Mr. Allison was a well-known Montreal financier.

In spite of almost all the men listed above having perished in the *Titanic*, the notion that somehow the rich were favored for escaping the sinking ship while the lower classes died continues to persist to this day.

TITANIC 1912

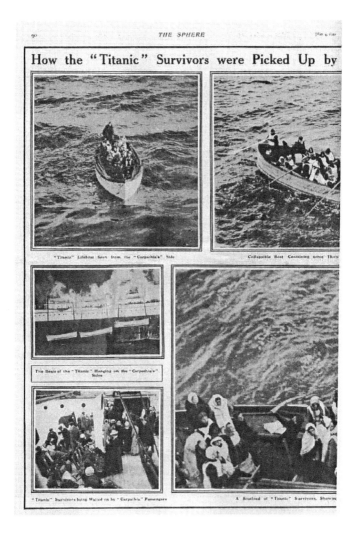

April 27, 1912] *THE SPHERE* 71

THE AFTERMATH OF SORROW : How the Tragedy Came Home to Many a Householder in Southampton.

GENERAL OFFICES

AMERIC

DRAWN FOR "THE SPHERE" BY H. M. PAGET

THE SCENE OUTSIDE THE WHITE STAR OFFICES AT SOUTHAMPTON

A scene outside the White Star offices at Southampton as witnessed by our artist, who visited the grief-stricken town last Saturday. There was a painful contrast between delight and black despair as anxious relatives or friends of those who had sailed on the "Titanic" recognised the long-sought names posted up on the official list while others sought in vain. Not until the board containing the last fateful list of survivors had been removed did the devoted watchers leave the offices. Over 600 relatives of drowned members of the crew attended a memorial service in St. Mary's Church on Sunday. It is estimated that there are fully 2,000 dependents of the crew in this town

Chapter Thirteen – "Beach her?"

Oddly enough when considering the history that took place one hundred years following the Titanic disaster is this short article which appeared *in The Baltimore American* on Tuesday, April 16, 1912.

SEA TWO MILES DEEP

Bottom Far Below Surface Where the Titanic Foundered.

Halifax, April 15. The deathbed of the $10,000,000 steamer *Titanic* and of probably many who must have been dragged down with her is two miles, at least below the surface of the sea.

The calculation was made by an official of the government Marine Department, who finds that depth on the marine chart at a point about 500 miles from Halifax and about 70 miles south of the Grand Banks, where he believes the Titanic went down. This location is midway between Sable Island and Cape Race and in line with those dangerous sands, which however, might have proved a place of safety had there been time to run the Titanic there and beach her.

***

Now we know that the captain of the *Costa Concordia* first hit underwater rocks on a reef in an area where he had no business sailing his ship off the coast of Italy on Friday, the 13th of January one hundred years after the Titanic disaster. In the *Concordia* tragedy, the ship either was intentionally beached on a reef or was steered there, with the result that the ship didn't "beach" but instead capsized with the loss of thirty-two lives.

The argument can be made that ninety-nine percent of those on the *Concordia* survived but had the captain not taken them for a dangerous joy-ride close to the island, none of them would have died that night.

One survivor of the *Titanic* told of her experience in leaving the sinking ship in lifeboat number thirteen, which she said would always be a lucky number for her the rest of her life.

She said that at about 3 am that they saw lights and had hope of rescue but those hopes were dashed when it turned out the lights were simply the "northern lights".

Then hope arrived at about dawn.

"As we neared the *Carpathia* we saw in the dawning light what we thought was a full-rigged schooner standing up near her".

They soon realized that the schooner was an illusion and simply a massive iceberg. She stated that they had to row around more ice bergs to get to the *Carpathia.*

Chapter Fourteen- Col. Astor, Notable & Hero of Titanic

While much of the news coverage dealt with the reports of women who saw Col. Astor, Maj. Butt and Capt. Smith all supervising the loading of women and children into lifeboats, some saw them stand by as the lifeboats pulled away from the sinking ship.

The Baltimore American told its readers on Tuesday, April 16th: **Col. ASTOR ON HONEYMOON**

Was Returning Home With His Bride, Who Was Miss Force.

Colonel Astor and his bride were returning from a prolonged honeymoon spent abroad. He was married to Miss Madeline Force last September. His marriage created much discussion, and there was trouble obtaining a minister to officiate. He had only been acquainted with his bride a few months before the marriage.

Colonel Astor was the son of William Astor and was born at his father's estate at Fern Cliff, near Rhinebeck-on-the-Hudson, July 18, 1864. After graduating from the scientific department of Harvard in 1888, he spent considerable time abroad. He received a thorough training in the management of the great Astor interests and was ready to exercise supervision when the death of his father in 1892 placed him at the head of his family.

He began the extensive building operations that added vastly to the princely fortune entrusted to him. He built a big addition to the Waldorf Hotel on the site at Thirty-Fourth Street and Fifth Avenue and later put up the St. Regis and the Knickerbocker. In his earlier manhood, Colonel Astor displayed a strong mechanical bent and turned out a patent bicycle brake, a pneumatic road scraper, a patent turbine and several other practical inventions.

Colonel Astor's first wife was Miss Ava Willing, of Philadelphia. She divorced him in 1909. Soon after the decree was granted a storm came up over the Caribbean, in which Colonel Astor was cruising with his youthful son and for almost two weeks nothing could be learned of his whereabouts, with the result that the wireless started flashing in every direction and the government went out to look for the Nourmahal, the Astor yacht. Eventually the news was brought by the skipper of a Red D steamer that the Nourmahal had been laying snugly in the harbor of San Juan, P.R. while all the fuss was being made about her.

The various holdings of the Astor family included the Astor Hotel which stood near Times Square until the 1970's.

Mrs. John Jacob Astor, who survived the Titanic disaster.

The Titanic at Ireland.

THE SPHERE

AN ILLUSTRATED NEWSPAPER FOR THE HOME

With which is incorporated "BLACK & WHITE".

Volume XLIX. No. 639. [REGISTERED AT THE GENERAL POST OFFICE AS A NEWSPAPER] London, April 20, 1912. [WITH SUPPLEMENT] Price Sixpence.

THE GREATEST WRECK IN THE WORLD'S MARITIME HISTORY—THE LOSS OF THE "TITANIC"

The above composite picture is given not as an actual document but as some realisation of essential factors in the loss of the great White Star fleet. Seeing that she sank at 2.20 a.m. on Sunday night no actual records of the vessel meeting with the ice are likely to be forthcoming. The icebergs shown here are reproduced from photographs obtained off Newfoundland. The size of them of course varies very considerably according to the season. The height of the vessel's bows above water-line would be about 60 ft. The opening shows near the top was a cable socket for a bow hawser, used when entering harbour.

Chapter 15 – Women Were Told Ship Could Not Sink; Wealthy Women Saved by Sacrifice of Men

The myth that the *Titanic* could not sink was key to convincing many of the women to board lifeboats and leave behind their husbands. This account from the *Los Angeles Times* tells of one woman who had hopes of seeing her husband even on the Carpathia. But she didn't.

Assured Until the Last Titanic Couldn't Sink.

By Jessie Leitch.
(By Direct Wire to The Times.)
New York. April 20.—[Exclusive Dispatch] About midnight Mr. Harper, the Rev. Dr. John Harper, came to my stateroom and told me that the vessel had struck an iceberg. While I was dreaming he went to learn further particulars and returned to say that orders had been given to put on the lifeboats. I did so. Picking up Nana, his daughter, in his arms he took her up to the deck. There, the women were ordered to the upper deck. I had to climb a vertical iron ladder, and Mr. Harper brought Nana after me up the ladder and the men at the top lifted her up to me again.

There was no opportunity for farewell and, in fact: even then we did not realize the danger, as we were assured again and again that the vessel could not sink, that the *Olympic* would be alongside at any minute and that the women and children were to be put into the boats first and the men to follow and that there were

boats sufficient enough for all. Our boat was well manned and it was the eleventh to leave the vessel.

After about half an hour, the *Titanic* went down. We were about a mile away, but even then I hoped and expected that Mr. Harper was in on one of the other boats. Many of which reached the *Carpathia* before ours did. How eagerly I looked for his face on the deck as we approached that vessel, but when all the boat-loads had come aboard I feared the worst.

The last day we spent on the *Titanic* was Sunday. Mr. Harper asked me to read the chapter at our morning family prayers and later we went to the Sunday morning services. The day was quietly and pleasantly spent and when Nana and I went to look for Mr. Harper at about 6 o'clock to go to dinner. I found him earnestly talking to a young Englishman whom he was seeking to lead to Christ. That evening before we retired, we went on deck, and there was still a glint of red in the west.

I remember Mr. Harper saying, "It will be beautiful in the morning."
We then went down to the staterooms. He read from the Bible and prayed and so he left us.

From *The Times Dispatch*, Richmond, VA, Thursday, April 18, 1912:

Wealth and Position Have No Precedence in Rule of the Sea

Some of the Women Whose Lives Were Saved Through Men's Self-Sacrifice

Women Saved in the *Titanic* Disaster, Now Aboard the *Carpathia*

Miss E. W. Allen

Lady Cosmo Duff Gordon
Mrs. J. W. M. Cardoza
Mrs. William E. Carter
Mrs. John Jacob Astor
Mrs. Jacques Futrelle
Miss Marie Young
Mrs. Tyrrel W. Cavendish
Mrs. John Thayer
Mrs. George D. Widener
Mrs. Paul Schubert
Mrs. Daniel W. Marvin

Mrs. J. J. (Margaret) Brown, who would forever be known as the Unsinkable Molly Brown. She had but three men in her lifeboat: one was old and useless, one was frozen and useless and one, a crewman at the tiller was a coward and useless.

Chapter Sixteen – Shut Up, Big Money!

The controversy over whether or not the news of the *Titanic* disaster was intentionally held back as a result of payoffs of the *New York Times* to Marconi officials was fully examined by a competitor of the *Times, the New York Herald.*

New York Herald, April 21, 1912, page 1:

'Keep Your Mouth Shut; Big Money for You,' Was Message to Hide News

Hold Story for 'Four Figures,' Marconi Official Also Warned the Carpathia Operator, While Anxious World Waited Details of Disaster.

While the world was waiting three days for information concerning the fate of the Titanic, for part of the time at least, details concerning the disaster were being withheld by the wireless operator of the steamship Carpathia under specific orders from T. W. Sammis, chief engineer of the Marconi Wireless Company of America, who had arranged the sale of the story.

This was admitted yesterday by Mr. Sammis, who defended his action. He said he was justified for getting for the wireless operators the largest amount he could for the details of the sinking of the ship, the rescue of the passengers and the other information the world had waited for.

The first information concerning the loss of the *Titanic* came Monday evening, and it was known at that time the survivors were on board the *Carpathia*. About midnight the first of the list of survivors began to come by wireless, and from that time until Thursday night, when the rescue ship arrived in port, the world waited and waited in vain for the details of how the "unsinkable ship" had gone down.

Three messages were sent to the *Carpathia* telling the operator to send out no news concerning the disaster. Two of these were unsigned, and the last one had the signature of Mr. Sammis.

"Keep Mouth Shut; Big Money."

The first message was unsigned, and it is said it was sent as a list of names of survivors were being forwarded. It read:--

"Keep your mouth shut. Hold story. Big money for you."

The messages from the Carpathia to the Marconi office concerning this matter were not available, but there was evidently some communication, for the second unsigned message followed after an interval. This message read:--

"If you are wise, hold story. The Marconi Company will take care of you."

The third and last message was addressed to **"Marconi officer, the Carpathia and the Titanic,"** and signed **"S. M. Sammis,"** chief engineer of the Marconi Company of America. This one read:-

"Stop. Say nothing. Hold your story for dollars in four figures. Mr. Marconi agreeing. Will meet you at dock."

Mr. Sammis was at the Waldorf-Astoria yesterday at the hearing before the sub-committee of the United States Senate, and he was asked about the message.

Mr. Sammis Resents Criticism.

"It is reported," he was told, "that a message was sent by you to the wireless operator on the *Carpathia* to which you gave the orders or at least said to him not to give out any details of the sinking of the *Titanic*, as you had arranged for four figures."

"Well?" he said is a defiant way.

"Did you send such a message?"

"Maybe. What of it?" he replied.

"It would be interesting to know if you actually sent such a message."

"Yes, I sent the message, but whose business is it?" Mr. Sammis asked with some heat.

"Perhaps it was no one's business," he was told, "but it is interesting to know that when the world was horror stricken over the disaster and waiting for the news, that there were persons preparing to capitalize the suspense and had arranged for 'four figures.' "

"Do you blame me for this," retorted Mr. Sammis, as he backed up against the wall. "Do you blame me for getting the highest price I could for the operator for the story he had to tell about the collision and the rescue. I thought I was doing a good turn for him, and I can't see how it is the business of anyone."

***

It is not unlikely that the sending of these messages with the apparent result that no details of the disaster came from the relief ship will form part of the inquiry that is being made by a sub-committee of the Senate. Part of this inquiry has been directed as to why a message from President Taft asking for information about Major Archibald W. Butt was unanswered, and it is not unlikely that in view of the message from Mr. Sammis that this will be taken up again.

Navy Likely to Have Records.

While these messages were intercepted by more than one wireless receiving station, there is one place where the Senate Committee could undoubtedly get copies of them. The New York Navy Yard has a powerful receiving station, and has what is known as an "intercepted message" book. These messages are considered confidential and are never given out, but the book would undoubtedly be at the disposal of the investigating committee.

Senator Smith said yesterday that the authorities in Washington knew on Thursday long before the *Carpathia* arrived, that the White Star line was contemplating the return of part of the Titanic crew to England by the steamship Cedric, and this information undoubtedly came from a government station.

John W. Griggs, one time Attorney General of the United States and Governor of New Jersey, is president of the Marconi Wireless Company of America. He said last night he had not heard that the chief engineer of the company was marketing the information of the disaster.

"This is a matter which will be looked into," he said. "I know nothing about it, had not heard of it before, and, of course, and cannot say what will be done until it is brought to my attention in an official way."

New York Herald, April 22, 1912, page 5:

TOLD TO 'KEEP OUT' NAVY MAN CHARGES

Wireless Operator Aboard Cruiser Declares the *Carpathia*'s Man Ignored President's Request.

[SPECIAL DISPATCH TO *THE HERALD*.]

PHILADELPHIA, Pa, Sunday.--That the *Carpathia* had not only refused to give the United States scout cruiser Chester information concerning the Titanic, but had told her wireless men to "keep out," was the statement made to-day by Frank Gaffney, chief operator of the *Chester,* now at League Island.

The refusal to answer, Gaffney declared, was after the *Carpathia* had been informed that President Taft was anxious to learn the fate of Major Butt and other prominent persons. Commander Decker, who was in charge of the cruiser, said the statements made by Harold Bride, that the navy operators were "wretched" was absurd.

The *Chester*, it is said, continued to flash questions to the *Carpathia* until the operators aboard the latter were compelled to answer because the high power of the navy's apparatus made the reading of messages to other points impossible.

"We made an effort to learn about Major Butt," said Gaffney, "and the only reply we got was 'keep out.'" Gaffney declared that he and Frank Blackstock, the other operator aboard the Chester, probably would be witnesses before the Senate committee.

Gaffney declared that the operators on board the Carpathia left them under the impression that all had been saved. He said that at one time they did answer when inquiries were made for Major Butt by saying "He

is not here."
One of the officers on board the *Chester* said this afternoon.—

"The operators of the *Carpathia* ignored everything that Gaffney and Blackstock sent or asked. Gaffney has been a wireless operator for more than six years, while Blackstock has been one for about three or four years. The former is capable of sending about forty-five words a minute and to say they are slow and wretched is absurd."

Titanic wireless operator Harold Bride is assisted up the gangplank from the *Carpathia* upon arrival in New York following the sinking of the Titanic.

The Titanic in May of 1911 prior to installation of her funnels.

Titanic's Lifeboats On Deck Of Carpathia

THE TRANSMITTING APPARATUS—HOW IT IS ARRANGED

Chapter Seventeen – Ode to the Titanic

From an unsigned editorial in the *Daily Graphic of London* on April 20, 1912:

We thought of that unforgettable message speeding through the viewless air that is marked upon the chart sheets S.O.S.

We picked up the common phrase of the operator and repeated to ourselves: "SAVE OUR SOULS," and thanked Providence for their salvation.

We pictured the scene. The lonely operator, composed with that old English valiance that has turned the blood of history into wine, calmly tapping out the cry of help.

We saw the realization of that message in the operator's cabin on other vessels.

We saw the wonderful chain composed of those three words, stronger than stone or iron or tempered steel, stronger than wind or sea, suddenly dragging all the vessels within the sphere of hearing away from their allotted course, and sending them on the great adventure of succor and mercy.

We pictured them racing along the railless roads of the open sea, rushing with insensate speed towards the spot of the catastrophe.

We had leisure to imagine the scene, because we were told there had been great deliverance: because we felt that man had fought his battle with the ocean and had won.

Then we knew that we had lost.
--- And what we learnt.

All the world knows how slowly those confessions of defeat came in upon us, how slowly the last flicker of an expiring hope was beaten down within our breasts, with what dilatory hands the veils were drawn from the implacable face of doom. Gradually the hush laid hold upon us; gradually a realization of what had happened sank into our souls.

We knew that nothing but a miserable residue of the great human freightage had been saved to us.

We knew that the enchanted floating palace conceived by the brain of man and wrought by his hands, with all its mighty scheme of luxurious ease, health, and comfort, lay somewhere tangled in old sea forces, two miles beneath the quiet surface of the sea. Little more do we know as I write. We can only hear the sobbing of the women at the street corners of Southampton, and find them in an eternal echo of the cheers with which we sent the Titanic out on her first, last, her only voyage.

Picturing that last dark awful moment, the last order of the captain, the last farewells --- so different from those we exchanged at Southampton --- the last tears and the last high human courage, all our sorrow is tempered by the thought that the women are alive to us and the children, and that the men died as we would have them die, as we should like to have died ourselves had God steeled our hearts with a similar courage.

Knowing this, as we peer into the dark picture of hat yet unrecorded scene, so deep with human anguish and yet so lighted with human grandeur, we may learn to endure the sobbing's of the women and the cries of the fatherless that come up to us in the surge of the immemorial sea.

Knowing this, we may take comfort in the great cry of a great poet in a sea-washed island that had born so many poets, and acclaim with him that:

Nothing is here for tears, nothing to wail,
Or knock the breast, no weakness, no contempt,
Dispraise or blame, nothing but well and fair,
And what may quiet us in a death so noble.

Icebergs and the "Titanic":

The Size and Shape of North Atlantic Bergs.

A NORTH ATLANTIC BERG SHOWING PROJECTING SHELF AND CRACK

On the extreme right the berg has a projecting arm or shelf probably extending under water for some distance further. It is on some such shelf that it is believed the "Titanic" struck. The arrow indicates the position of a huge crack. One member of the "Titanic's" crew states that there was "a lot of ice" on the liner's deck. A man was also seen running up to some passengers with a piece of ice in his hand saying, "Will you believe it now?" Had such a scene as is here shown been incurred by the vessel's contact the results might have been still more sudden and disastrous

Portion of Iceberg Falling into the Sea

This view was obtained in the North Atlantic at the very moment when a large piece of ice and some loose snow spun is was falling into the water

A LARGE BERG WITH A STEAMER IN CLOSE PROXIMITY—AT ST. JOHN'S, NEWFOUNDLAND

The above direct photographic view gives a good idea of the size and shape of North Atlantic icebergs. A recent witness at the American inquiry states that the height of the fatal berg was 60 ft. Between 50 ft. and 100 ft. were the dimensions given in last week's "Sphere." Here is a tendency to believe that the dimensions of the berg must have been far too dramatic than those mentioned, but there is no doubt on the other hand that a height of 60 ft. does not connote a very large berg (see dimensions given in account above)

Chapter 18 – One Hundred Years of Getting the Story Wrong

The following news article about the *Titanic* appeared on Sept. 22, 2010 in the *New York Daily News* and consists of "new information" that the Titanic sunk due to human error, not due to an iceberg.

Human error really sank the Titanic, not an iceberg, granddaughter of ship's second officer claims

BY MICHAEL SHERIDAN
DAILY NEWS STAFF WRITER
Wednesday, September 22, 2010

Forget the iceberg, human error was the real cause behind the sinking of the *Titanic.*

This surprising claim comes from the granddaughter of the ocean liner's second officer, Charles Lightoller.

"It just makes it seem all the more tragic," Louise Patten told *London's Daily Telegraph* on Wednesday. "They could easily have avoided the iceberg if it wasn't for the blunder."

Patten spilled the beans on the long-held family secret in advance of the release of her book, "Good as Gold," which is not about the Titanic but weaves in elements of the incident as she remembers it.

The mistake, which led to the sinking of the massive vessel in 1912 and killed 1,517 people, occurred when a steersman "panicked."

"The real reason why *Titanic* hit the iceberg, which has never come to light before, is because he turned the wheel the wrong way," Patten said.

Once the mistake had been made, she added, "they only had four minutes to change course and by the time [first officer William] Murdoch spotted [Robert] Hitchins' mistake and then tried to rectify it, it was too late."

Patten said her grandfather, the most senior officer to survive the sinking, covered up the error for fear it could ruin White Star Line, the company that own the ship, as well as the reputations of his fellow sailors.

Lightoller, however, was not present when the error occurred, Patten noted. He heard of it during a meeting afterwards.

After the *Titanic* struck the iceberg, she said, her grandfather believed the mighty vessel sank faster than it should have because J. Bruce Ismay, chairman of White Star Line, pressured the ship's captain to keep sailing.

"If Titanic had stood still, she would have survived at least until the rescue ship came and no one need have died," Patten said.

With News Wire Services

***

Author's Note: There is no evidence that any of the claims of this news article are correct and plenty of witness testimony to the contrary. For example, the engines were shut down almost immediately due to the infusion of water into the engine rooms. Also, there is no evidence that Ismay had any conversations with the Captain about any issues, including the need to continue the ship to keep sailing. The apparent motivation underlying the article was simply the need of the granddaughter of Lightoller to cash in on her family legacy by selling books. The reporter and *The Daily News* which published the article failed its readers and showed that the passage of one hundred years hadn't really improved journalism in New York. As for the incredible statement that "no one need have died" ignores the fact that had every lifeboat been filled the survivor count may have been around 900. There simply were not enough lifeboats and the closest ship to the *Titanic* was the *Californian*, which had turned off its wireless. The captain of the *Titanic* failed to set off the rockets in the correct distress mode and therefore its message was not understood. The *Titanic* did come to a standstill and immediately began to sink after the long cut was made in her hull by the iceberg.

The *New York Daily News* wasn't the first and sure won't be the last publication to continue to introduce incorrect information to its readers. The March, 2012 edition of the *Smithsonian* provided a fairly factual account of the story of Dorothy Gibson. Unfortunately, the editor of the *Smithsonian*, Michael Caruso, provided a "From the Editor" introduction to the *Titanic* coverage in his magazine. Caruso's first sentence read: **"One hundred years after an innocent iceberg was struck by the world's most famous ocean liner, we find ourselves riding the latest wave of Titanic obsession".**

Not to be too picky with the *Smithsonian* editor who must be a very busy fellow, it's kind of difficult to understand how an inanimate object like an iceberg can be "innocent" or even "guilty" of anything. In addition, the *Titanic* was not the world's most famous ocean liner when it struck the iceberg. The ship became famous for hitting the iceberg and sinking with over 1500 casualties but up until that time, it simply was the newest and largest, but not the most famous.

As Caruso attempts to provide a new and novel theory of the theme of perception as to "why the lookouts didn't spy the lethal iceberg", Caruso and his writers failed to research the facts and witness testimony before the American and British investigating committees.

At both of the probes the lookouts stated clearly that they had not only seen the icebergs but had reported the icebergs three times to the First Officer, Mr. Murdoch, who failed to take action until fifteen minutes later, when it was too late.

Frederick Fleet testified that had he had binoculars he would have sighted the iceberg in time for the ship to swing clear of the ice but he insisted that 3 warnings were given and ignored.

The binoculars had been taken ashore at Queenstown, Ireland by the prior crew and Fleet said that **"they told me there wouldn't be any glasses"** in his testimony before the U. S. Senate Commerce Committee which held hearings three days after the disaster.

It appears that the *Smithsonian* writer and editor had a "cool" idea for a novel explanation of the disaster that simply wasn't rooted in the facts or history. For this article entitled "Fateful Encounter" to have been published and misinform so many young minds is a travesty. The topic of visual perception at sea is a very real problem for any sailor on almost any body of water and experienced sailors will gladly avoid night travel in small vessels, if possible. Large vessels have the equipment to aid them in navigation. But for the *Titanic*, it is clear, lookouts had but one job, to look out and to warn and they did.

As for Caruso characterizing the iceberg as "lethal" when in his first sentence he had labeled it as "innocent" shows that the iceberg had acquired quite a sinister nature in just a few paragraphs. It was the ship that collided with the iceberg which was simply following a course proscribed to it by Mother Nature. And it's not nice to fool with Mother Nature.

Titanic lookout Frederick Fleet survived; he testified at the British hearings that he had given three warnings of ice ahead.

Supplement to The Sphere, April 27, 1912] *THE SPHERE* iii

TERED THE LUXURY OF THE "TITANIC."

THE READING AND WRITING ROOM ON BOARD THE "TITANIC" NOW IN THE DEPTHS OF THE ATLANTIC

The size and equipment of the *Titanic* was such that it was not rare for the minds of the passengers to quickly realise that the water benefited nature in which they had been spending a pleasant evening at the cabins in which they were enjoying the last hour of sleep would soon be sinking beneath them. Everything was at first quite leisurely. Colonel Gracie says that when the vessel struck "the passengers were not alarmed, but asked over the matter. The few who appeared on deck had

taken time to dress properly." Several of the sole survivors were in the smoking-room at the time of the contact with the berg. It was probably the liveliest public room at the moment. There would also probably have been no use as two quiet readers sitting in the saloon drawn above, scanning the pages of a novel before turning in. There had been more than 2,340 persons on board; of these no fewer than 1,635 perished.

April 27, 1912]   THE SPHERE   71

THE AFTERMATH OF SORROW : How the Tragedy Came Home to Many a Householder in Southampton.

THE SCENE OUTSIDE THE WHITE STAR OFFICES AT SOUTHAMPTON

A scene outside the White Star offices at Southampton as witnessed by our artist, who visited the grief-stricken town last Saturday. There was a painful contrast between delight and black despair as anxious relatives of friends of those who had sailed on the "Titanic" recognised the long-sought names posted up on the official list while others sought in vain. Not until the board containing the first batch of the list of survivors had been removed did the devoted workers leave the offices. Over 1000 relatives of drowned members of the crew attended a memorial service at St. Mary's Church on Sunday. It is estimated that there are fully 1,000 dependents of the crew in the town.

Chapter Nineteen

- Titanic Mania Includes the Absurd and Conspiracy Theories

The U. S. News & World Report ran an article in 2010 about the *Titanic.* With a dramatic decline in circulation, the once proud news magazine has found a way to penetrate modern society and added more to the confusion and mayhem about the *Titanic* by publishing these strange and somewhat idiotic remarks from their readers. Instead of critiquing the article, this chapter will simply provide some of the reader comments which were published at the end of the USN&WR story. The reader comments go a long way to explain the current state of affairs in America.

The comment from "Eric" just about sums up the sanity level of the comments below.

While spell check was used to clean up the comments for spelling, no software program exists to cleanse copy for insanity or stupidity. Keep an eye out for a few glimmers of understanding about the true story of the Titanic.

Are you Muppets serious?
Eric 8:09 PM July 10, 2011

The *Titanic* was a beautiful ship, it was a lie how they said it was unsinkable but i suppose it wasn't meant to sink all we have to do is to know it's still there the sadness of those who lost their lives

Rihanna 6:04 AM June 09, 2011

I think there is no man left who saw the accident at that time. I think the main reason of *Titanic* sank is the carelessness of the staff. Like we saw in the *Titanic* the staff was too busy to see the kiss of Jack & Rose. Like that the staff may not give concentrate in their job so it happens.

Upendra 3:50AM May 11, 2011

Maybe there were dinosaurs in that time and might of hit the ship a couple of minutes before they hit the iceberg and thought it was the iceberg cause they were trying to turn so fast away from it that they didn't notice and maybe not it's just a theory no one person will ever know the truth I think that's a sad story and movie to tell and watch so I feel bad for all the people but we have to think that maybe there was or maybe it wasn't strong or maybe it was really strong but the iceberg was really even bigger than anyone remembers.

Kristina of MN 7:19PM May 10, 2011

No one will ever know the true story of the *Titanic*. We may make things up, but in the end of all of it, it isn't true. Why make stuff up? Like it's not right to tell people what didn't happen or what isn't true. We really only know that it hit an iceberg and sank. That's it. So why must crap up about how great it was. Was it really great? Or was it crappy?

Gillian of MA 9:58AM April 29, 2011

This is a very sad story of the *Titanic*. But they shouldn't just be blaming one person for this disaster! Because in my opinion I think it was the crews fault and not just the captains. Plus when they were putting people on lifeboats they let the High Class and Middle Class go first and that's why many of the people that died were Low Class. I actually kinda know the true story about this from my great great great (I don't know how many greats though) grandma that was aboard on the Titanic but I only know about it very roughly. What I know is that the Titanic wasn't all that fancy because a lot of people told tall tales about how awesome or spectacular it was. And 2nd thing I know is that it was the person who controls the radio or whatever because before the Titanic crashed it received commands from other ships to not sail the way they were going but the person controlling the radio didn't believe it and he just didn't tell the captain. So I don't know a lot about it but trust me there are a lot of tall tales or myths about what really happen on the Titanic. And to tell you the truth no one can really tell us the true story of the Titanic and those who could have took those memories with them to their grave. I'm really interested in finding out the true story of it because I actually think that my great3 grandmas could have twisted the tale up before actually telling my mom what it really was. So if you guys have more information on these please tell me. Ok thanks

    Anita of CA 8:27PM April 26, 2011

    The *Titanic* isn't strong because it would've went over a small iceberg.

    Rohit of OH 10:38PM April 21, 2011

    I have fully agreed with Breanna of WV opinion about *Titanic* sinking. At that time there is a great difference between lower class and higher class people in the society. So Higher class people get the first choice to enter in to the life boats, at the same time they was not agreed and force the ship crews to allow the lower class people to enter into the life boats. Naturally life boats were not filled to their capacity, So many people who are lower class has died.

Adinarayan 2:00 AM April 16, 2011

Titanic was a really cool ship which was called the ship of dreams. A lot of people died because they stayed with their husbands and might have thought the people who were giving the news were probably lying. *Titanic* lifeboats can hold up to 65 people. A lot more people would have been saved if the officers filled the lifeboats up more than what they did.

Breanna of WV 6:23PM April 15, 2011

I HAVE TO AGREE TOTALLY WITH JENNIFER FROM TN.

JAMES of AZ 4:17PM April 04, 2011

This was the worst thing ever.
Ashley cox of IN 2:32PM November 08, 2011

It was a beautiful ship, so sad.
Bob of MN 12:15AM October 18, 2011

How did the *Titanic* sink on the TV news.
Tyler   12:54PM October 16, 2011

Wow!!!!!!!!
Lily of VA 8:03AM October 13, 2011

People like to believe that things cannot happen so they conjure up conspiracy to make sense of it all. The fact is when you have 48,000 tons of ship moving at 22 knots that is a hell of a lot force. It hit the berg at an angle that caused the riveted plating to collapse. It's all about pressure. By the way, that wasn't an ice cube *Titanic* struck it, was an ice berg that dwarfed the *Titanic* in size and weight. Really it all makes sense to me. The true reason *Titanic* sank was the crew's complacency to include the overconfident Capt. E.J. Smith.

Eric of TX 5:28PM August 17, 2011

So how do you know that they had switched the ships and dubbed the *Titanic* the *Olympic* and the *Olympic* the *Titanic*? I have been interested in the Legacy of the Titanic since I was a child. Since then I have researched nearly every document about Her and Her sister the *Olympic* and I have found no information, anywhere saying that the White Star Line switched the Sister ships. Also after both accidents with the *Olympic* they DID manage to repair the ship by taking a propeller from the *Titanic* and scrapped some metal off of her in 1911 this is far from her completion in March the following year. So why would they switch a completed ship with a non-completed ship, that COULD be repaired?

Robert of NY 2:20PM August 14, 2011

When you have an iceberg rip a gash along a large portion of your hull, even the best built ship is going to sink. Most conspiracy theories are ridiculous, but the *Titanic* Nuts go far beyond into the realm of lunatics!

Roger of OR 1:35PM August 14, 2011

Titanic wasn't *Titanic* it was *Olympic,* its twin sister. The owner of White Star liner swapped the ships but why. Because when *Titanic* was still being made the *Olympic* went out. But it had 2 crashes the 1st not too bad. But the 2nd was bad the platen was burst and so were the bolts. One of the propellers was ripped off. And worse the keel was bent. The owner decided it was too much money and too long to fix so they just patched it up, that was temporary fix. The *Olympic* was on cruises. So they swapped ships. So when the *Olympic* hit the iceberg which people thought it was Titanic, it hit the temporary fix and it had no chance? And it sunk.

Eddie of CA 7:39AM August 08, 2011

It happened because of carelessness, after facing the iceberg, if the ship was moving.

Why did the captain go so fast? Could there be a conspiracy about the sinking? Smith was a Jesuit. He was visited by a high up Jesuit official prior to the voyage. I believe *Titanic* was built by Protestant Irishmen. 3 very wealthy men were coaxed and pleaded with to go on this maiden voyage. I'm rough on the names, John J Astor, Guggenheim I think and a guy named Strauss. These men opposed the making and forming of the Federal Reserve. They died and months later at Jeckle Island a small group of men formed the Federal Reserve.

John of UT 7:18PM April 03, 2011

Robert Hitching, the helmsman of the *Titanic* panicked at the moment he saw the iceberg ...of course many people had different thoughts. Robert saw the iceberg diagonally on his left hand side, so he could have just kept on going straight and avoiding the loss of 1,500 people. However the captain of the ship thought that the iceberg was small, so he just wanted to go straight through it with the biggest ship in the world...the truth is that on the top the iceberg was only half a meter, however what they didn't see was the huge ice under the water that was 190 meters tall.

John of AL 1:50AM March 18, 2011

I think it was because a lot of the people on the ship failed to listen to the other ships call out saying that they had sailed through those same waters a couple hours ago and there were a lot of icebergs there and to approach with extreme caution ...people in the radio room didn't inform the captain or anybody else for that matter about what the other ship had told them...and also even before all this the captain had had several wrecks just prior to sailing the *Titanic* so i think there are a lot more people here to blame than just one and also my personal opinion this might not have happened in the first place if they had boasted against God saying that even he couldn't sink it because I believe that God can do anything but apparently some people don't believe that which kinda sucks. Wish they did.

Jennifer of TN 3:14PM March 05, 2011

I am amazed that *Titanic* is bigger than one island

Samana of DE 12:02PM February 18, 2011

According to me it's the captain's mistake because he should not have sailed the boat in almost maximum speed keeping in mind that it's mostly an ice covered ocean.

Mohan 6:54PM February 14, 2011

How can you be so sure it was definitely the ice berg of because of which the titanic sank, what evidence was found to support this statement.

Abigail of 3:07PM December 19, 2010

This is interesting. There are a lot of points in here, but I think the main reason why *Titanic* sank is because she ran into the iceberg at top speed. Going that fast back then, any ship would have sunk.

Alex of WA 12:59AM December 19, 2010

Some experts recently found that *Titanic* erodes rapidly during the years.

How can we conclude safely that its weakness point was its structural material?

Panagiotis 6:01PM December 06, 2010

If the *Titanic* had hit the ice berg head on it may have stayed afloat

AJ of SC 1:10PM November 22, 2010

From reader comments to Titanic International Society:

Stolen Cup Up for Sale!

Colin said:

My father in law and I have a genuine 1st class egg cup which was taken off the *Titanic* by a steward before it left for the maiden voyage.

It is what the collectors call the wisteria pattern in the turquoise color.

It is in lovely condition and states Stonier and Co and is dated 03/1912.

Is there a collector who may be interested in it?

We paid a lot of money for it some years ago and it comes with a note of its history.

Many thanks in advance.

Religious Bigotry Sunk Titanic

Kathy said:

TITANIC 1912

Hello-I grew up hearing my Mother's story of the Titanic. You see she was 12 years old living in Belfast with her family when her Mother would tell her the story of the Titanic and how it would never reach America because of all the Protestant Blasphemy that went on while building the Titanic. You see in Belfast during that time it was the Protestants that got most of the jobs-very few Catholics were hired. However, my Grandfather was a Master Carpenter on the Titanic even though he was Catholic. He built a chest and a mirror from unused wood from the Titanic which has been handed down to me.

Wealth and Position Have No Precedence In Rule of the Sea

THE SPHERE

The Need for Searchlights on Ocean Racers.

HOW POWERFUL HEAD LIGHTS COULD BE FITTED TO LINERS

Chapter Twenty –

French Liner Dodged Ice on Same Path

The April 17, 1912 edition of the *New York World* included an article in which the Captain of a French steamship, the *La Bretagne*, talked about how his ship dodged ice for seven and half hours just prior to the crossing of the *Titanic*.

"The ice was everywhere," said Capt. Mace today when *La Bretagne* came into the harbor. The French ship had run the same steamship lanes as the *Titanic* and did so about ten hours ahead of the doomed liner.

"The file of huge bergs as far as the eye could carry to the north and west looked like the New York skyscraper line."

By the description of conditions prevailing at almost the exact spot where the *Titanic* met her death blow and from fourteen to ten hours before the *Titanic* herself drew up on the ice menaced territory, Capt. Mace gave today what was considered by marine experts almost conclusive evidence that the *Titanic* must have rammed one of the giant bergs head on and not, as had been surmised by some, run onto an almost submerged floe.

The whole zone of ice over seventy miles extent, and from which *La Bretagne* had to sheer off to prevent being crushed, was bristling with great detached bergs. Capt. Mace counted more than forty of the floating ice crags. One berg, which was 650 feet high, was photographed by a passenger *on La Bretagne* from a distance of two and one-half miles.

A second element injected into the problems surrounding the conjectural cause of the disaster to the

Titanic arises from Capt. Mace's description of the weather in the vicinity of the waters wherein the *Titanic* was overwhelmed. The sky was clear during all the time that La Bretagne was passing through the zone of ice, according to Capt. Mace, and there was not any time sufficient fog to obscure the presences of the towering pinnacles ice. As far as the horizon those aboard *La Bretagne* could distinguish the serried spires of the ice masses, unveiled by the fog which traps ships.

The first explanation for the *Titanic*'s fatal blunder advanced by seamen was that the weather must have been thick and that the berg which was to deliver the death stab to the great White Star liner had shrouded itself in a fog of its own making.

Capt. Mace said today that he entered the ice area at 7 am on Sunday morning and that for five hours he was skirting a great mass of detached bergs and ice fields.

"The ice covered the sea as far as the eye could reach," said Capt. Mace. "It was the greatest floe that I have ever seen. At first we moved through small ice and floes almost awash. Before we left the field, which we had been skirting to avoid trouble, we were able to count forty large bergs. At many times there were so many great bergs in the field of vision at the same time as to give the impression of New York's skyline from the lower bay."

Accord to *La Bretagne's* log, the ice field was drifting from about 50 west longitude and 41 north latitude to 51 and 42 longitude and latitude respectfully. This would bring the great field within the radius of the *Titanic*, which followed the French ship twelve hours later.

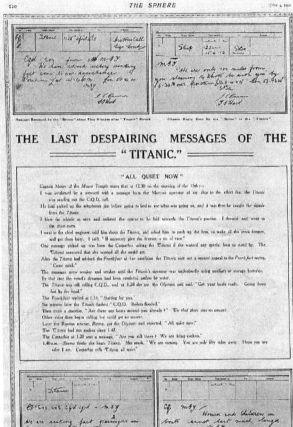

THE LAST DESPAIRING MESSAGES OF THE "TITANIC."

"ALL QUIET NOW"

Captain Moore of the *Mount Temple* states that at 12.30 on the morning of the 15th:—

I was awakened by a steward with a message from the Marconi operator of my ship to the effect that the *Titanic* was sending out the C.Q.D. call.

He had picked up the telephones just before going to bed to see what was going on, and it was then he caught the signals from the *Titanic*.

I blew the whistle at once and ordered the course to be laid towards the *Titanic's* position. I dressed and went to the chart-room.

I went to the chief engineer, told him about the *Titanic*, and asked him to push up the fires, to wake all the extra firemen, and get them busy. I said, "If necessary give the firemen a tot of rum."

One message picked up was from the *Carpathia* asking the *Titanic* if she wanted any special boat to stand by. The *Titanic* answered that she wanted all she could get.

After the *Titanic* had advised the *Frankfurt* of her condition the *Titanic* sent out a second appeal to the *Frankfurt* saying, "Come quick."

The messages grew weaker and weaker until the *Titanic's* operator was undoubtedly using auxiliary or storage batteries. By that time the vessel's dynamos had been rendered useless by water.

The *Titanic* was still calling C.Q.D., and at 1.20 she put the *Olympic* and said, "Get your boats ready. Going down fast by the head."

The *Frankfurt* replied at 1.33, "Standing for you."

Six minutes later the *Titanic* flashed "C.Q.D. Boilers flooded."

Then came a question, "Are there any boats around you already?" *To that there was no answer.*

Other ships then began calling but could get no answer.

Later the Russian steamer, *Birma*, got the *Olympic* and reported, "All quiet now."

The *Titanic* had not spoken since 1.47.

The *Carpathia* at 1.20 sent a message, "Are you still there? We are firing rockets."

1.40 a.m.—*Birma* thinks she hears *Titanic*. She sends, "We are coming. You are only fifty miles away. Hope you are safer I am. Carpathia calls *Titanic at speed*."

Coffins being offloaded from the cable ship MacKay-Bennett in Halifax where 153 of the victims are buried.

Chapter Twenty-One

Heroic Actions of Captain & Officers

Bulletin From *Carpathia* Indicates That Probably Not More Than 600 Passengers Are Among the 705 Survivors Nearing This Port Aboard the Cunarder, Leaving 1505 Dead

(Special to the Evening World)

BOSTON, April 17 – *The Globe* prints the following special cable this afternoon from P. T. McGrath, the *Globe*'s correspondent in Newfoundland.

ST. JOHNS, N. F., Via North Sydney, N.S. April 17. --- From an absolutely well authenticated source comes the report that the captain, officers and crew of the *Titanic* displayed unexampled bravery in the face of the most appalling marine catastrophe in the world's history, endeavoring to maintain order, quell the panic, launch and man boats and embark the passengers, assuring all there was no immediate danger while fully cognizant that they would soon be plunged beneath the waves with their fast sinking ship.

Capt. Smith and all the principal officers heroically stuck to their posts to the end, encouraging directing and assisting to the extent of carrying fainting women and children from the decks and berths to the gangways and helping them to the boats, returning, even when the waves were practically submerging the ship, to the rescue of passengers, absolutely regardless of self. They worked like Trojans while it was possible to save a single one of the passengers, while death, sure and swift, stared them in the face.

It is said that the captain and every officer, except the six who manned the boats with the subordinate members of the crew, went down with the ship while life was within their reach, if they had disregarded their duty to the passengers and escaped, they alone knowing how near the ship was to sinking after striking the iceberg.

Confirmation of the report that reached New York this morning stated that the *Carpathia* has only about 700 survivors of the *Titanic* disaster aboard was received this afternoon at the office of the Cunard Line. The message is from Winfield Thompson of the *Boston Globe*, a passenger on the *Franconia* of the Cunard Line. The *Franconia* is now off the coast of Nova Scotia. Following is the message:

THE *FRANCONIA* ESTABLISHED WIRELESS CONNECTION WITH THE CARPATHIA AT 6:20 O'CLOCK THIS MORNING, NEW YORK TIME. THE CARPATHIA WAS THEN 498 MILES EAST OF AMBROSE CHANNEL LIGHT IN

NO NEED OF ASSISTANCE, STEAMING 13 KNOTS, AND EXPECTS TO REACH NEW YORK AT 8 O'CLOCK THURSDAY EVENING. SHE HAS A TOTAL OF 705 SURVIVORS ABOARD.

THE FRANCONIA IS RELAYING PERSONAL MESSAGES FROM THE *CARPATHIA* TO SABLE ISLAND.

This message is the first authentic information that has come from the *Carpathia* since 9 o'clock yesterday morning. It increases the number of dead in the disaster to 1,505. Undoubtedly there are at least 100 sailors from the *Titanic* on the *Carpathia* among the survivors, so there cannot be more than 600 passengers saved.

NUMBER OF PASSENGERS SAVED ABOUT 600

Inasmuch as no word has been received from Capt. Rostron of the either to his own line or to the White Star line since his report of about 600 survivors, the latest information is accepted in steamship circles as representing the true state of affairs on the Carpathia. And if the number of passengers saved is under 600, as Mr. Thompson's message indicates, there must have been many women drowned, judging from the names of men in the list of survivors.

The Cunard Line has notified the Department of the Treasury that no newspaper reporters will be allowed to board the *Carpathia* until she reaches her pier. This is to avoid the disturbance to the survivors of the *Titanic* disaster, many of whom are doubtless hysterical from grief.

The following telegram was received at the Navy Department in Washington from Commander Decker of the scout cruiser Chester, via Portland, Me.:

Carpathia states that list of first and second-class passengers and crew were sent to shore. *Chester* will relay list of third-class passengers when convenient to *Carpathia.*

The message is taken to mean that the list transmitted by wireless from *Carpathia* to the station at Cape Race, N.F., through the *Olympic* contains the names of all the first and second-class passengers rescued.

The latest report from the *Carpathia,* via the *Franconia*, effectually disposes of the report that 868 survivors were picked up. *The Evening World* has consistently held to the figures sent out from the only authority from which such figures should come – Captain Rostron, of the *Carpathia*. The last report does not materially change *The Evening World's* information, because there is still ground for belief that the *Carpathia' s* report to the *Franconia* did not include the *Titanic's* seamen who were saved.

The dead, according to the best information available concerning the number of persons aboard the *Titanic,* number 1,505. Doubtless one of the *Titanic's* officers-of whom six are said to be among the survivors-has the ship's manifest, the purser's books and other documentary evidence of the number of passengers and crew on board and the names of all the ship's company.

A relay private message from the *Carpathia* received here today announced that "all the women are safe".

The message was received by Mrs. J. W. Bonnell, of Youngstown at the Waldorf from Henry Wick, her brother who is aboard the *Olympic*. Wick received a wireless from his niece, Mrs. Bonnell' s daughter, Caroline Bonnell, who with George W. Wick, her uncle, sailed on the *Titanic*. The message read: "All the women safe. Have no word of George."

George Wick's name does not appear on the list of survivors on the *Carpathia*, and he is believed lost.

The Captain and crew of the Carpathia were awarded a loving cup by the survivors of the Titanic to thank them.

The news boys hawk papers on the streets of New York.

BALTIMORE, WEDNESDAY MORNING, APRIL 17, 1912. 16 PAGES PRICE ONE CENT

TITANIC WAS RIPPED OPEN IN HER CRASH WITH ICEBERG

The first authentic details of the terrible wreck of the Titanic were flashed in a wireless message from the steamer Bruce.

The Titanic, going at 18 knots an hour, struck a submerged spur of a great iceberg.

The vessel's decks were ripped open and the upper works of the ship came crashing down like giant hail.

The ship's compartments from amidships forward were speedily flooded.

Many tons of ice fell upon her decks, contributing to the demolition and confusion.

There were painful scenes as the women and children were lowered into the boats.

The number of survivors of the Titanic disaster on board the Carpathia was given as 808.

The second, third, fourth and fifth officers and the second Marconi operator were the only officers on the Titanic reported saved.

The revised death toll was placed at 1,302.

The Carpathia is picking its way through ice fields to New York.

The scout cruisers Chester and Salem were sent to meet the Carpathia and give assistance if necessary.

Tearful crowds swarmed the offices of the White Star Line in New York.

London, Paris and New York were grief-stricken and overwhelmed by the news of the disaster, and tearful crowds thronged the steamship offices in all three cities, waiting hour after hour for news.

Upper Works And Boats Smashed And Shower Of Debris Fell Upon The Decks.

BRUCE FLASHES DETAILS

Terrible And Pathetic Scenes Enacted As Those Leaving The Ship Took Their Allotted Places In The Boats---Death Toll, 1,302, Saved, 868, Are Latest Estimates.

THE TIMES-DISPATCH: RICHMOND, VA., SUNDAY, APRIL 21, 1912.

1,500 People Were Not Drowned; They Were Foully Murdered

MAD CRAZE FOR SPEED HAS BEEN DISSIPATED

No More Will Great Liners Race Across Ocean as Effort to Set Up New Record—One Result of Titanic Lesson.

CABLE STEAMER THAT IS SEARCHING FOR TITANIC'S DEAD; HER CAPTAIN, CLERGYMAN ABOARD AND SOME SUPPLIES

REVIEW OF OCEAN'S GREATEST HORROR

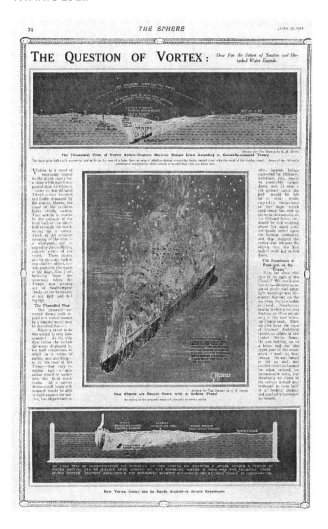

Chapter Twenty-Two – Don't Sink The Same Week as *Titanic* and Expect Anyone to Read About It!

From the *New York Evening World*

"SOS" FLASHED BY WRECKED LINER WITH 200 ABOARD

Rescue Ship Rushed to Canadian Liner, *Earl Grey*, Fast on Rocks.

HALIFAX, N.S. April 17 – Wireless messages for help from the Canadian steamer *Earl Grey*, which plies between Charlottetown, Prince Edwards Island and Piciou, N. S. were received this afternoon. She is ashore off Cape John and has 200 passengers aboard. The Government boat Minto has been sent for assistance.

It was reported late today that the *Earl Grey* had sunk after flashing the following message: "Need immediate assistance. Sinking."

PICTOU, N. S. April 17 – The Government steamer Earl Grey, from Charlottetown to Pictou, went aground at 10:30 this morning between Tony River and Cape John, according to a wireless message received here from the Grey. The Government steamer *Minto* from Pictou to Charlestown, which was anchored off of Caribou Harbor, has gone to the Grey's assistance.

The wireless message received from the Grey at 11:59 a.m. said she was ashore two miles west of Tony River on rocky bottom.

***

The *Earl Grey* wasn't a lucky name for a ship in Canadian waters as on June 24, 1917, another ship named

Earl Grey, a schooner, ran aground off Halifax harbor and sank.

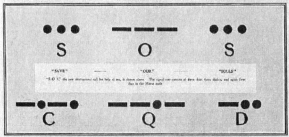

A LAST VISION OF THE "TITANIC" BY NIGHT—AN IMPRESSION AT CHERBOURG

DIAGRAM III.—HOW THE "TITANIC" GRADUALLY SAN

Chapter Twenty-Three

– Marconi Denies Reports of Ordering Wireless Operators to "Keep Mouths Shut"

From The Washington Times, April 25, 1912:
MARCONI TESTIFIES HE DID NOT TELL WIRELESS MEN TO KEEP THEIR MOUTHS SHUT

DID NOT TRY TO BLOCK NEWS, HE SAYS

**Expresses Regret that Information Was Withheld
SMITH ASKS HIM SCORES OF QUESTIONS**

Operator Got $500 for Story of Titanic Disaster

By John Snure
The grilling of Guigielmo Marconi, the great wireless expert, on the subject of whether the Marconi Company exercised a censorship of the news of the loss of the Titanic, before the arrival of the Carpathia in New York, was the feature of the morning session of the Senate Subcommittee, which is investigating the facts as to the recent disaster.

It is doubtful if ever in the career of the suave Italian, whose wizardry of the wireless is known the world over, he was put in a more embarrassing position than when plied with questions by Senator Smith about the part he is alleged to have taken in ordering the operators on the Titanic to "Keep your mouths shut".

MARCONI TESTIFIES HE DID NOT TELL WIRELESS MEN TO KEEP THEIR MOUTHS SHUT

GUIGLIELMO MARCONI,
Inventor of wireless telegraphy, who tells Senators how system operates.

DID NOT TRY TO BLOCK NEWS, HE SAYS

Expresses Regret That Information Was Withheld.

SMITH ASKS HIM SCORES OF QUESTIONS

Operator Got $500 for Story of Titanic Disaster.

By JOHN SNURE.

The grilling of Guiglielmo Marconi, the great wireless expert, on the subject of whether the Marconi Company exercised a censorship of the news of the loss of the Titanic, before the arrival of the Carpathia in New York, was the feature of the morning session of the Senate subcommittee, which is investigating the facts as to the recent disaster.

It is doubtful if ever in the career of the suave Italian, whose wizardry of the wireless is known the world over, he was put in a more embarrassing position than when plied with questions by Senator Smith about the part he is alleged to have taken in ordering the operators on

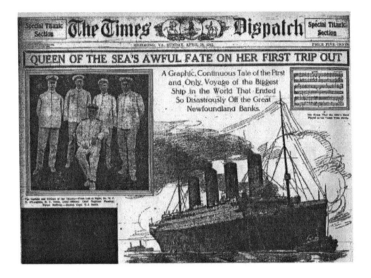

Chapter Twenty-Four

– Saved by the Wireless!

From Baltimore American April 17, 1912:
SAVED BY THE WIRELESS
Remarkable Record Made by the Latest Great Discovery.

The Titanic disaster and the quick aid brought to the sinking leviathan by the wireless, again brings forth the name of Marconi; one of the greatest benefactors of mankind. The wireless system has already saved thousands of lives at sea, it has been instrumental in the capture of criminals who, were they not taken into custody, might have wrought much harm, and it has increased the means of communication between countries and between ships flying different flags that it has helped to knit more closely the bonds of friendship between various nations, thus tending toward greater peace in the world.

Before the echo of the collision between the iceberg and the monster ship had died away, the wireless instrument was sputtering its call for help – a call that was sent to the North, the East, the West and the South – a call that was picked up and translated by scores of ships and numerous land stations.

As the electric flashes were received on the keys of the ships and land stations, no time was lost, but rudders were turned, and before operators could tap out an answer to the Titanic's signal of distress, several vessels were on their way to the Titanic's signal of distress, several vessels were on their way to the rescue.

Successful operation of wireless dates back to 1899, when Marconi, the great inventor of this now necessary equipment for all ships, established communications between the steamship St. Paul, the first ship equipped with a wireless apparatus, and a station on the English coast, with a distance of about 70 nautical miles between the instruments. The world heard of this in amazement at the time but none believed that within the space of 10 or 12 years they would see this invention clicking off messages between points 10,000 miles distant. It was not realized that this invention would, in the near future, be instrumental in saving thousands of lives.

But it fell to Jack Binns – whose name is now known all over the world – wireless operator on the steamship Republic to make the world fully appreciate the real value of Marconi's invention.

Binns' opportunity came on January 23 1909, when the Republic, with over 400 passengers, was rammed off of No Man's Land, below Nantucket, by the steamship

Florida. As the large hole was rammed into the side of the *Republic* and her hold began to fill with water, causing her to sink, Binns, in the wireless-room, tapped out the message – the shriek of the wireless – "C. Q. D." The liner *Baltic*, one of those which went to the rescue of the *Titanic* yesterday, was one of the first to receive this signal of distress, and the Baltic's operator communicated with Binns and learned the state of affairs. All the passengers and crew were saved.

Shortly after this instance came the collision between the steamship Ohio and an iceberg off the Pacific Coast. George C. Eccles, the wireless operator, sent the cry of distress, and was still calling for help when the water was a few feet from the lower deck of the ship. The 250 men on board were saved, but Eccles, who stuck to his post to the last minute and who was caught in the little wireless room, was drowned.

The rescue of those on board the *Meridia* and the *Admiral Farragut*, which collided off Atlantic City; of those on the Merchant and Miner's steamship *Lexington*, which struck a hurricane on the way to Galveston, and numerous other rescues at sea record the feats of the wireless and the heroism of the wireless operators. Again, the passengers and crew on the *Ontario*, the Merchants and Miner's ship which caught fire off Montauk Point about two weeks ago, were saved by the flashing of Marconi's invention.

There is a law compelling all seagoing vessels to be equipped with wireless, but it is in a measure, unnecessary. The absolute necessity of the equipment is realized and no vessel is considered complete without it.

Chapter Twenty Five

The Money Boat?

One of the lifeboats left without being full, while others were also only partially filled with passengers and crew, one in particular stood out. That one was the subject of a first-person account by first-class passenger Laura Francatelli. She wrote of hearing "an awful rumbling' after the *Titanic* hit the iceberg. Francatelli worked as a secretary for wealthy baronet Sir Cosmo Duff-Gordon and his wife Lady Lucy Christiana and was aboard the ship on its fateful voyage.

Francatelli told of boarding one of what she believed to be one of the last lifeboats which was only was occupied by five passengers and seven crewmen. This account really doesn't make too much sense as other witness testimony during the official hearings and other survivor accounts refer to the partially occupied lifeboats as having been the first ones to be launched. By the time the last boats were being put off the ship, it was clear to everyone that the ship was going to sink and there was a great clamor to gain a seat in a lifeboat, with men being shot to keep them from jumping in the boats.

With the trauma the young woman was going through at the time it is understandable that she would have confused not only the order of the boats being loaded but just about anything else that night. What seems unmistakable are two parts of her story: one that the boat was loaded far below its capacity and the second that the boat did not go back to pick up those who flung themselves into the ocean and were screaming for help. *The Daily Mail* had this account last year, pointing out that Francatelli, died in 1967 and that her family was going to auction off her recollections in 2011.

In hindsight the lifeboat the party boarded was rather controversial.

As she confirms in her own words, there were more crew on board than passengers and room for potentially 40 or 50 more people who could have been saved.

***

'There was also great controversy surrounding Sir Cosmo because when they arrived in New York he gave the seven crew members £5 each.

'There was one train of thought that he was being very kind and generous and was compensating the men for the items they lost in the sinking. Certainly that is what Miss Francatelli thought.

'But the payment was also interpreted as blood money at the time. Was he paying the men for a place in the lifeboat and his own life?'

There was yet another account of a lifeboat with few people aboard in which a wealthy American reportedly paid the crew to get away quickly from the Titanic with his family on board.

THE PASSING OF A GREAT JOURNALIST : *William Thomas Stead*

WILLIAM THOMAS STEAD, WHO WAS DROWNED FROM THE "TITANIC," APRIL 14, 1912

Los Angeles Sunday Times.

Over the Grave of the Brave

Who Died at Their Posts on the Titanic.

Chapter Twenty-Six
No Price on Lives Lost

From the *Chicago Times:*

TITANIC OWNERS NOT LIABLE FOR DEATHS ON SEA

If Precedent Is Followed Company Will Probably Settle for Property Loss Without Dispute, but Admiralty Lawyer Says it Cannot Be Held Further

(BY DIRECT WIRE TO THE TIMES.)

CHICAGO, April 16 – (Exclusive Dispatch) Relatives of the 1232 passengers who lost their lives in the wreck of the *Titanic* will be unable to collect a single dollar in damages, according to Charles W. Greenfield, of Kremer and Greenfield, admiralty attorneys with offices in the Fort Dearborn Building.

If the White Star line follows precedent, it will settle without legal dispute for the loss of property, but as this was insured the company will lose nothing on that score.

"There is no law which fixes liability for loss of life on the high seas," said Attorney Greenfield today. "About ten years ago several suits for loss of life were filed in the Federal court here, but they were dismissed because of the lack of any statute fixing liability.

"Suits for loss of property very seldom follow disasters of this kind. The steamship companies are usually covered by insurance and in the past all have generally settled without going to court."

Mr. Greenfield added that some states and nations have laws fixing liability for loss of life in wrecks, but that they are not applicable to the high seas. The *Titanic* was on the "high seas" at the time it foundered.

It is estimated that the passengers on the *Titanic* carried in money, bonds, jewels and other securities approximately $6,000,000.

TITANIC 1912

THE SPEED OF THE GREAT LINERS : A Factor

ONE AND A QUARTER TIMES HER OWN LENGTH IN HALF-A-MINUTE—DOTTE

"ICEBERG RIGHT AHEAD, SIR!"—IF THE OBSTACLE WERE 741 YARDS AWAY AT THE

The two scale illustrations give an idea of the speed of the ill-fated "Titanic," which it will be remembered is considered a slow boat against the force of the Cunard line and the latest big liners observing the illustrations that after the look-out men in the crow's-nest have observed the obstacle it but half-a-minute of time the huge vessel would have sped forward 740 over and a quarter of the "Titanic" may have been half-a-kn

THE MECHANISM BY WHICH THE BOATS WERE LOWERED.

A PAIR OF THE WELIN DAVITS ON BOARD THE "TITANIC"

The Welin davit, which was fitted to the "Titanic," and is also found on a large number of the latest type of passenger liners, is the ingenious invention of Mr. Axel Welin. The davit is carried over the side by turning the cog-wheel screw, seen in the centre of the picture. The bottom of the machinist is a cog which, working on a base point, forms a double action, thus throwing the davit outwards to its extreme limit in a matter of moments. The old type davit has to be completely turned in two operations which take a considerable amount of time.

Chapter Twenty-Seven

"The Titan" Foretold Fate of Titanic

Daily Mail, London, England, April 17, 1912

Forecast Fulfilled.

Strange Prophecy of the Titanic's Fate.

How strangely imagination may anticipate history has seldom been more remarkably shown than in the disaster to the Titanic. It was foretold in many of its details in a curious little novel by Mr. Morgan Robertson entitled "Futility," published in the United States fourteen years ago. The story tells how a monster liner, the Titan, "was the largest craft afloat and the greatest of the works of men. In her construction and maintenance were involved every science, profession, and trade known to civilization." She was believed to be "unsinkable, indestructible." She carried 2,000 passengers, and she started on her voyage across the Atlantic in April.

She was running at full speed when "a shout from the crow's nest split the air. 'Ice,' yelled the lookout, 'ice ahead. Iceberg. Right under the bows.' The first officer amidships and the captain, who had remained there, sprung to the engine room telegraph....In five seconds the bow began to lift, and ahead and on either hand could be seen through the fog a field of ice which arose in an incline 200 feet high in her track." There was a "deafening noise of steel scraping and crashing over ice...Forty-five thousand tons—deadweight—rushing through the fog at fifty feet a second had buried itself at an iceberg.

"Had the impact been received by a perpendicular wall the elastic 'resistance of bending plates and frames would have overcome the momentum with no more damage to the passengers by a mere shaking up, and to the ship than the crushing of her bows and the killing to a man of the watch below. She would have backed off and, slightly down by the head, finished the journey at reduced speed.

"But a low beach, possibly formed by the recent overturning of the berg, received the Titan, and with or keel cutting the ice like the steel runner of an ice boat and her great weight resting on the starboard bilge she rose out of the sea higher and higher—then she heeled, overbalanced and crashed down on her side to starboard."

Titanic under construction at Harland & Wolff in Belfast.

The docks were crowded with thousands at the Cunard terminal in New York waiting for the Carpathia to arrive with the survivors.

Chapter Twenty-Eight

Going Down in the Sea

Los Angeles Times, April 16, 1912

The Times provided this list of major ship disasters up to the sinking of the Titanic:

Great Marine Disasters of History and Lives Lost.

1859-Lady Elgin (Lake Michigan)   Sunk   297

1890-Shanghai   Burned   300

1891-Utorsia   Collision   563

1892-Nanchow   Foundered   [500]

TITANIC 1912

1893-Warship Victoria   Collision   358

1894-Horn Head   Sunk by Iceberg   62

1895-Chicora   Vanished in Lake Michigan   38

1895-Warship Reigns Stagina   Collision   400

1895-Coltma   Wrecked   171

1895-Copernicus   Sunk   153

1897-Kapunda   Foundered   300

1898-La Bourgogne   340

1904-General Siceum   Burned 253

1904-Norge   Wrecked on a reef   730

1905-Hilda   Sunk   123

1906-Valencia   Foundered   119

1906-Sirto   Foundered   326

1906-Brazilian Cruiser Aquidaban   Sunk   213

1907-Larchmoot   Lost   135

1907-Hong Kong   Struck rock   130

1907-Berlin   Wrecked   125

1907-Lakota   Struck a reef   unknown

1907-Columbia Collision   100

1908-Matau Maru   Collision   250

1908-Star of Bengal   Wrecked   310

1909-Seyne   Sunk

1910   Marquette   Sunk

1910-General Chaney   Wrecked   136

1910-Prince Wilbelm   Sunk

1910-Tecsuro Maru   Wrecked

1911-Santa Rosa   Sunk   20

1911-John IrwinSunk   11

1912-Titanic   Wrecked by Iceberg   (est.) 1500

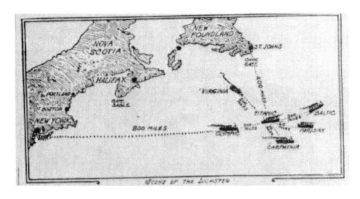

This map shows the position of the Titanic at about 430 miles south of Newfoundland when it struck the ice berg.

The Carpathia arrives in New York.

Chapter Twenty-Nine

328 Bodies Found

Baltimore, Maryland newsman H. L. Mencken was well suited for the times of the trans-Atlantic liner competition as well as the competition to cover the news of the Titanic. Here are some fairly representative quotes of Mencken:

All successful newspapers are ceaselessly querulous and bellicose. They never defend anyone or anything if they can help it; if the job is forced on them, they tackle it by denouncing someone or something else.
H. L. Mencken

A cynic is a man who, when he smells flowers, looks around for a coffin.
H. L. Mencken

From the Marine Museum of the Atlantic at Halifax:

The strategic position of Halifax made it the base for cable ships which repaired breaks in the underwater telegraph cables connecting Europe and North America. The White Star Line turned to these ships to search for bodies. Their tough crews, used to working in rough seas and ice, were ideally suited for the grim task.

A boat crew from the Cable Ship *Minia* picks up one of the *Titanic* victims. Recovery was hard, grim work, amidst large waves and dangerous ice floes. Crews were paid double and given extra rum rations.

Before the survivors even arrived in New York, the first cable ship left Halifax to search for bodies. With coffins, 100 tons of ice, an undertaker and a chaplain, *Mackay-Bennett* left on April 17, arriving on-site three days later. She found 306 bodies, so many that embalming fluid ran out and 116 had to be buried at sea.

Another cable ship, *Minia*, departed Halifax on April 22, *relieving Mackay-Bennett* and finding another 17 bodies.

The Canadian Government lighthouse supply ship *Montmagny* left Halifax on May 6, and found four bodies.

A Newfoundland sealing vessel, *Algerine*, sailed on May 16 but found only one body, steward James McGrady, the last to be recovered. In total, 328 bodies were found.

Twelve hundred were never recovered, some sinking with Titanic, others being dispersed by currents, bad weather and ice.

Nova Scotia was no stranger to White Star Line shipwrecks, as the SS Atlantic sank near Halifax in 1873 taking over 500 lives. For the 209 *Titanic* bodies that came to Halifax, the Deputy Registrar of Deaths, John Henry Barnstead improvised a remarkable identification system.

Bodies were numbered as they were pulled from the sea and personal effects were bagged. Further details (tattoos, clothes, jewelry) were noted and photographs taken at the temporary morgue in the Mayflower Curling Rink.

A body is fished from the sea.

The cable ship Mackay-Bennett returns to Halifax with recovered dead of the Titanic. The ship ran out of supplies for embalming and had to conduct burials at sea.

Coffins are unloaded from the cable ship Mackay-Bennett

A recovered body is prepared by an embalmer on the MacKay-Bennett.

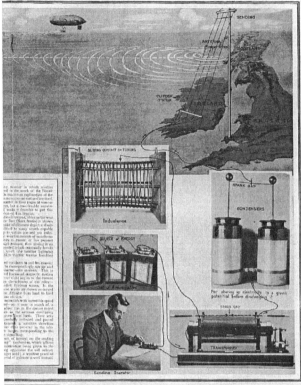

[April 27, 1912] THE SPHERE 71

THE AFTERMATH OF SORROW : How the Tragedy Came Home to Many a Householder in Southampton.

THE SCENE OUTSIDE THE WHITE STAR OFFICES AT SOUTHAMPTON

Chapter Thirty

Agonizing Wait for Relatives of Crew

SOUTHAMPTON IS GRIEF STRICKEN
SCENES OF ANQUISH IN HOME TOWN OF *TITANIC* CREW
Harrowing Stories of Misery That Will Follow Deaths of Bread Winners - Hundreds of Tearful Women Besiege Offices of White Star Line

(BY DIRECT WIRE TO THE TIMES)
SOUTHAMPTON (Eng.) April 16. (Exclusive Dispatch)
The town is completely staggered by the colossal extent of the *Titanic* disaster. Never have such pathetic scenes been witnessed in Southampton. It seemed impossible to realize the fact that the *Titanic* now lays a shattered wreck at the bottom of the Atlantic as and yet the full significance of the disaster to hundreds of homes in Southampton has not made itself apparent.

A large proportion of the crew is resident here. There are already harrowing stories in the numerous households, which will lose breadwinners, and of the enormous misery which will follow in the train of the terrible disaster.

Hundreds of tearful women, most of whom had husbands, fathers, brothers, sons or sweethearts on the wrecked vessel, stood hour after hour in Canute Road and the terminus of the Terrace where the offices of the White Star line are situated, eagerly scanning the latest bulletins hoping against hope that every hour would be bring brighter news.

Everywhere there is evidence of the appalling tragedy, many public bodies have issued expressions of sympathy, flags are flying at half-mast on shipping companies' offices and numerous engagements of a public character have been cancelled. Public anxiety is momentarily increasing.

The crowds around the White Star offices are bearing the agonized tension bravely, women in their uncomplaining misery eagerly waiting the publication of the list of crew for which the local manager of the White Star has cabled New York. If necessary, the offices will be kept open throughout the night, so that latest tidings may be circulated.

From the London Times April 16, 1912:

KING AND QUEEN HORRIFIED AT "APPALLING DISASTER"

(BY A. P. NIGHT WIRE TO THE TIMES)

LONDON, April 16 --- King George has sent the following message to the White Star company:

"The Queen and I are horrified at the appalling disaster which has happened to the Titanic and at the terrible loss of life. We deeply sympathize with the bereaved relatives and feel for them in their great sorrow with all our hearts ---George R. and I".

The Queen mother, Alexandra, has sent a message of sympathy to the company, in which she says:

"It is with feelings of deepest sorrow that I hear of the terrible disaster to the Titanic and of the awful loss of life. My heart is full of grief and sympathy for the bereaved families of those who have perished."

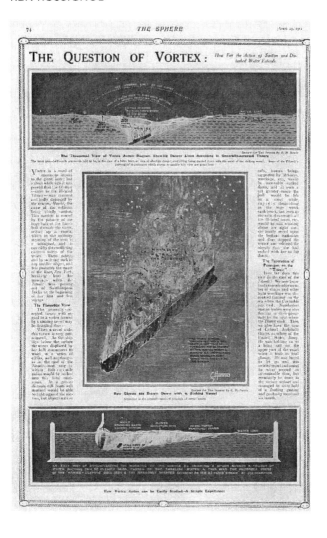

Chapter Thirty-One

LIFEBOATS TO SAVE ALL ORDERED NOW BY ISMAY

From The New York Evening World, April 20, 1912
Vessels of International Mercantile Marine Now Being Equipped So That Every Passenger and Sailor May Have Chance for Life

J. Bruce Ismay, Chairman of the Directors of the International Mercantile Marine, announced today that orders had been issued to equip all vessels of the lines embraced in that corporation with a sufficient number of lifeboats to carry all passengers and every member of the crew. The orders go into effect immediately and Mr. Ismay said the work of completing the equipment was already under way.

The lines affected by the order are the White Star, American, Red Star, Atlantic Transportation, Leyland and Dominion. The order was prompted by the experience of the International Mercantile Marine in the foundering of the Titanic.

"We have learned by bitter experience," said Mr. Ismay, "although our ships have been equipped with respect to life saving apparatus in full compliance with Admiralty Laws."

Supplement to The Sphere, April 20, 1912 THE SPHERE

The GREATEST WRECK in the WORLD'S HISTORY

The LOSS of the WHITE STAR LINER, "TITANIC."

Which sailed from Southampton on Wednesday, April 10, and was totally lost off Newfoundland on Sunday night (April 14)

NOW LYING TWO MILES DEEP IN THE ATLANTIC—THE "TITANIC" (TONNAGE 46,000)

Harrowing.

SOUTHAMPTON IS GRIEF STRICKEN.

SCENES OF ANGUISH IN HOME TOWN OF TITANIC CREW.

Harrowing Stories of Misery That Will Follow Deaths of Bread Winners—Hundreds of Tearful Women Besiege Offices of White Star Line.

[BY DIRECT WIRE TO THE *TIMES*.]

SOUTHAMPTON (Eng.) April 16.—[Exclusive Dispatch.] The town is completely staggered by the colossal extent of the Titanic disaster. Never have such pathetic scenes been witnessed in Southampton. It seemed impossible to realize the fact that the Titanic now lies a shattered wreck at the bottom of the Atlantic, and as yet the full significance of the disaster to hundreds of homes in Southampton has not made itself apparent.

A large proportion of the crew is resident here. There are already harrowing stories in the numerous households, which will lose bread-winners, and of the enormous misery which will follow in the train of the terrible disaster.

Hundreds of tearful women, most of whom had husbands, fathers, brothers, sons or sweethearts on the wrecked vessel, stood hour after hour in Canute road and the terminus of the Terrace, where the offices of the White Star are situated, eagerly scanning the latest bulletins, hoping against hope that every hour would bring brighter news.

Everywhere there is evidence of this appalling tragedy, many public bodies have issued expressions of sympathy, flags are flying at half-mast on shipping companies' offices, and numerous engagements of a public character have been cancelled. Public anxiety is momentarily increasing.

The crowds around the White Star offices are bearing the agonized tension bravely, women in their uncomplaining misery eagerly waiting the publication of the list of the crew for which the local manager of the White Star has cabled New York. If necessary, the offices will be kept open throughout the night, so that the latest tidings may be circulated.

Silent film star Dorothy Gibson survived the sinking. She starred in the first movie about the Titanic, made in 1912. No copies of the movie survive to this day. She later was in Italy during WWII and was sent to a concentration camp by the Nazis.

KEN ROSSIGNOL

The first in the series of ships in the *Titanic* class was the *Olympic*.
She is shown here arriving in New York on June 21, 1911.

The third in the class was the *Britannic*, which was appropriated by
the British government for use as a hospital ship. It was believed to
have struck a German mine during WWI. It then sank in the Aegean
Sea.

Bruce M. Caplan is the world's leading authority on the Titanic. His book, The Sinking of the Titanic is available in Kindle and paperback at Amazon. The Privateer Clause photo

ABOUT THE AUTHOR

After covering hard news for 22 years while publishing a weekly newspaper, Rossignol sold the newspaper in 2010 and has begun devoting full time to writing and lecturing to audiences around the world about the *Titanic* and maritime history.

The story of the *St. Mary's Today* newspaper is now available in Kindle and paperback at Amazon: The Story of THE RAG! The book includes nearly 200 editorial cartoons that appeared over the years.

There are now two new books with scores of great short stories from *THE CHESAPEAKE*, a fun fishing and nonsense monthly publication which covers all manner of recreation, travel, fishing and hunting in and around the Chesapeake Bay and elsewhere in one endeavor produced with Cap'n Larry Jarboe. *The Chesapeake: Scales & Tales* and *The Chesapeake: Legends, Yarns & Barnacles*.

Rossignol also publishes the DWIHitParade.com.

The first in a series book, *The Privateer Clause* was released in 2010 and in 2011, *Return of the Sea Empress* hit the waves.

The third in the series now available at Kindle: Join Marsha and Danny Jones on the latest cruise of the Sea Empress as the ship traces the fateful route of the RMS Titanic 100 years following the disaster.

TITANIC – Flashback to 1912

Follow Titanic!
Marsha and Danny Jones star in this series, killing terrorists and enjoying lobster spaghetti on a sailboat off the coast of St. Vincent.

Follow Triangle-Vanish is the newest in the series of Marsha and Danny Jones thrillers.

Shopping in St. Thomas is dangerous and that's not counting the merchants.

The great new Chesapeake books all about fishing fun and nonsense, a collection of short stories by Rossignol and Cap'n Larry Jarboe have also been published in 2011. The books contain dozens of great tales and yarns including some of the best from Steve Uhler, Jack Rue, Frederick L. McCoy, Mel Brokenshire, Vi Englund, Alan V. Cecil, Alan Brylawski, Pepper Langley and more! More than you will ever want to know abounds in the volumes.

Also look for Larry Jarboe's FISHY DEALS! and his newest book: One Titanic Fish! You won't be disappointed! In Kindle and paperback at Amazon. Remember, to read the Privateer Clause series before you take a cruise! Cruising has never been more affordable, more fun and maybe, if you are lucky enough to board the Sea Empress, more exciting!

BOOKS BY KEN ROSSIGNOL

The Privateer Clause — Cruising has never

been more dangerous! This first in the series introduces Marsha and Danny Jones in a thriller that takes the *Sea Empress* through serious threats to every life on the ship!

RETURN OF THE SEA EMPRESS

— Would you want the President of the United States on your cruise ship? Find out what took place as the president joined the ship after the *Sea Empress* left Europe for Florida.

Follow Titanic --- One hundred years after the *Titanic* went to its grave, excitement and adventure awaits those on the *Sea Empress* as the ship suddenly diverts to a

northerly crossing of the Atlantic.

FOLLOW TRIANGLE – VANISH

The 4th in the series of Marsha & Danny Jones Thrillers as the *Sea Empress* heads for the Bermuda Triangle with the President's choice for the Supreme Court on board...what could possibly happen?

The Chesapeake: Tales & Scales is the first in the series of short stories that have appeared in *The Chesapeake* over the years. Join Jack Rue, Pepper Langley, Mel Brokenshire, Cap'n Larry Jarboe, Ken Rossignol, Vi Englund, Frederick L. McCoy, Stephen G. Uhler, Alan V. Cecil and Alan Brylawski as we explore the land of the flask, the fiddle and the dark roasted possum!

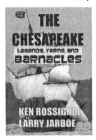

The Chesapeake: Legends, Yarns, & Barnacles --- The second in the series of short stories from the pages of *The Chesapeake*! Great fishing instructions wrapped in irony about sailing, boating and hunting. Littered with buzzards and lighthouses, the sagas of the tidewater region of the Chesapeake Bay and Southern Maryland will delight every reader!

The Story of THE RAG! — The true-life story of the *St. Mary's Today* newspaper—the small-town newspaper that won a landmark First Amendment decision that went all the way to the Supreme Court when a sheriff, state's attorney, and a posse of deputies cleaned out newsstands to keep voters from reading critical articles before voting. The decision, Rossignol v.

3

KEN ROSSIGNOL

Voorhaar, was issued by the Fourth Circuit United States Court of Appeals. Now available as an ebook, and in paperback with loads of great editorial cartoons!

BOOKS BY LARRY JARBOE

FISHY DEALS — Death awaits Commissioner Jerry Largent as he attempts to weave a great new way to power vehicles. Will he survive drug dealers and sneaky politicians?

One Titanic Fish

The second in the series of Fishy Deals.

Coming Soon by Larry Jarboe:

Snorkeling: Fun and Affordable!

(The Guide to Free Diving)

Books by Bruce Caplan

The Sinking of the Titanic

Now in its 18th printing in paperback, the 1912 original has been abridged and edited by the nationally known author Bruce M. Caplan. Caplan appears before audiences nationwide and lectures on cruise ships around the world on the *Titanic* disaster. The 100th Anniversary Commemorative edition is now in Kindle for the first time, due to popular demand!